Summer Every Day

Summer Every Day

Over 65 vibrant Mediterranean-inspired recipes to share with friends

Acland Geddes & Pedro da Silva

Photography by
Kate Whitaker

rps

RYLAND PETERS & SMALL
LONDON • NEW YORK

Dedication

This book is dedicated to all the staff at Megan's, past, present and future. Without you it's just bricks and mortar.

Senior Designer Megan Smith
Commissioning Editor Céline Hughes
Production Manager Gordana Simakovic
Art Director Leslie Harrington
Editorial Director Julia Charles

Copy Editor Laura Gladwin
Prop Stylist Jo Harris
Food Stylist Lucy McKelvie
Assistant Food Stylist Ellie Jarvis
Indexer Hilary Bird

Originally published in 2014 as *Friends Around the Table*. This revised reissue published in 2019 by Ryland Peters & Small
20–21 Jockey's Fields,
London WC1R 4BW
and
341 E 116th St
New York NY 10029
www.rylandpeters.com

10 9 8 7 6 5 4 3 2 1

ISBN: 978-1-78879-111-3

Printed and bound in China

A CIP record for this book is available from the British Library. US Library of Congress Cataloging-in-Publication Data has been applied for.

Note

Both British (metric) and American (imperial plus US cups) are included in these recipes; however, it is important to work with one set of measurements and not alternate between the two within a recipe.

contents

introduction

It's been nearly 20 years since I left school, and it really is quite remarkable how little of my education is still with me. As far as my memory is concerned, each subject is only really about one thing. Biology? Osmosis. Geography? Oxbow lakes. History? Turnip Townsend. It's not that I had a bad education – quite the opposite – it's just that all I really cared about was what my next meal was going to be. And the one after that. Oh, and what snack I would have during morning break, and which sweets I was going to buy while waiting for the bus, and… well, you get the idea.

I know that introducing a cookbook with the whole 'I've always been in love with food' routine is about as clichéd as it gets, but in this case it really is true. I just obsess over it. Parents don't nickname their child Baby Porker for nothing. I even get a kick out of spearmint toothpaste, for goodness, sake. It's a borderline psychological problem. Suffice it to say that I had to base my working life around food. After various attempts it was abundantly clear that an office job just wasn't going to do it for me. If I sat in front of a computer day after day it would only be a matter of time before I tried to eat it.

So, food it is then.

I won't bore you with the details of my culinary life before my owning my restaurant, Megan's, but I worked under a whole variety of chefs: nurturing ones, shouty ones, heavily drug addicted ones. Each one taught me something new, not just in terms of food, but also in terms of what it truly means to live and work in the restaurant business, and I owe a huge debt of gratitude to each and every one of them. There were, however, two lessons that eclipsed all the others.

First and foremost: cooking is not a science, it's an art, and it can be done by anyone. 'But I don't know how to cook, I'm useless in the kitchen,' people sometimes say. But there is no 'can' and 'can't' in cooking. One man's burnt is another man's crispy. Provided that it's actually edible (and it takes some effort to make something genuinely inedible), it's cooking. You just need to start experimenting and finding your way.

AU
PETIT CAFE

GARIBALDI
In the
GARDEN

Fine, you're probably not going to make a groundbreaking dish on your first attempt – but then again you might. A two-year-old might draw a stick man that's somehow more moving than a Renaissance fresco. Some of the most poetic English phrases I've heard have come from the mouths of non-English speakers. If a novice can create beauty through painting and language, why not through cooking?

Of course, this is a cookbook, and it therefore contains recipes, but they are there to teach you techniques and methods. To stick with the art analogy, they're just showing you which materials and colours tend to work well together. But you're not in prison; the recipe isn't the warden. You don't have to ask permission to swap an ingredient or furtively add a pinch of chilli when the book isn't looking. You're the boss, not me.

The second lesson I learned is so simple, but is so often overlooked by restaurants. It is responsible for the whole ethos of Megan's and, if I'm honest, its success also. Despite what most people think (and that certainly includes the majority of would-be restaurateurs), food is not the be-all and end-all. Of course it's important, but the ambiance and setting are equally so. If you don't feel relaxed, you won't enjoy your meal, no matter

how many Michelin stars you throw at the problem. Eating is about conviviality, sharing a laugh while topping up your neighbour's wine glass, carving up a chicken and arguing about who gets to eat the crispy skin.

I once heard someone describe a film as 'self-aware' and I thought it was about the most damning insult they could have given. But the more I think about it, the more I realize it applies to many restaurants. What we've tried to create at Megan's is a place where the customer's enjoyment comes first: a canvas of simple, good food and relaxed atmosphere where the diners can enjoy each others' company without the restaurant trying to muscle in and steal the limelight.

I hope you'll enjoy the recipes that Pedro da Silva, the fantastic head chef here at Megan's, and I, Acland Geddes, have put together. But what I hope most of all is that our recipes will give you the inspiration and confidence to get in the kitchen and start developing your own dishes.

Now, stop wasting your time reading this drivel. Roll your sleeves up and get involved!

lunch al fresco

OK, I'll admit that at first glance the concept of an al fresco dining chapter by a Brit sounds about as likely as a scuba-diving kit in the Sahara. What do us 'limeys' (or 'poms' or *rosbifs*) know about outdoor living? Isn't it all just sideways drizzle, stiff bowler hats and the occasional pagan ritual on a weekend? Well yes, we aren't blessed with all that much good weather, but I don't know of any other nation that relishes it as much as the British. The national mood shifts as soon as the thermometer hits 22°C (72°F). It's as if everyone's problems are somehow put on hold and swept under the carpet until the inevitable rain comes round again.

Along with the smiles and the renewed 'shall we get a dog?' discussions, there is an almost pathological need to eat al fresco. An unfortunate consequence is that people get so carried away with the excitement of eating outdoors that they forget about the food itself… I'm sorry, but half a supermarket baguette and a pot of unrefrigerated, waxy taramasalata isn't the 'fantastic picnic spread' I was promised, thank you very much. 'Come on, don't be such a sourpuss, we've got apples and crisps too!' Oh great, a handful of Pringles and a bruised Granny Smith. I'll remember that recipe next time you come over for dinner.

Just because you're feeling summery and relaxed doesn't mean your tastebuds have gone on holiday. The weather shouldn't be an excuse for throwing any old thing together, it should be a reason for taking extra care so that the meal can be a memorable one – because who knows when the next ray of sunshine will be seen around these parts?

Thanks to the amazing garden at Megan's, we've been practising outdoor-focused dishes for years. It's an oasis of calm in the middle of busy London. A huge wall of ivy starts vibrantly green in spring and turns a magical rust-red as summer draws to a close. The rose tree grows wild, affectionately brushing the customers' heads as they walk past. Of course I'm biased, but I really do think it's one of the most serene and beautiful eating spaces in the city. That said, it would be nothing more than a nice garden if it weren't for the food and the laughs that are enjoyed within its walls. Here are a handful of our favourite dishes, best enjoyed outdoors where and when possible!

This is about as refreshing as it gets. We often serve a shot glass of it on our antipasti platters, but it more than holds its own as a starter. It's not strictly authentic, but it also doubles up as one hell of a pseudo-Bloody Mary mix.

Gazpacho

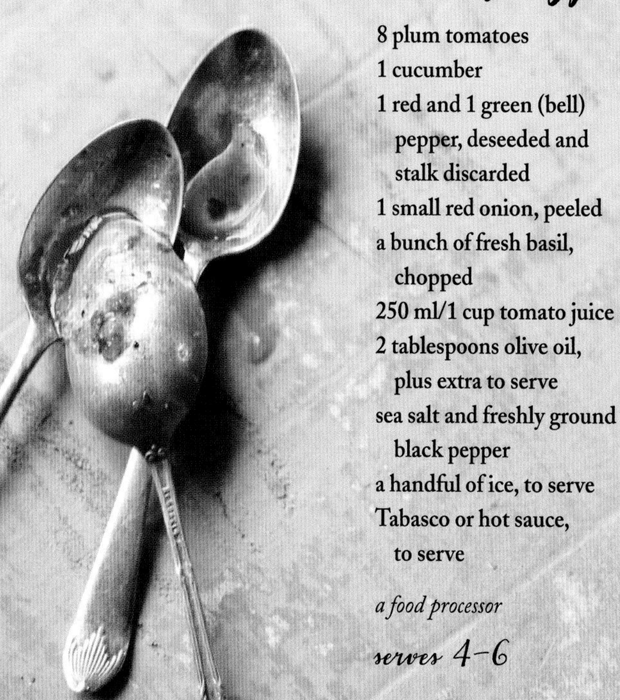

8 plum tomatoes
1 cucumber
1 red and 1 green (bell) pepper, deseeded and stalk discarded
1 small red onion, peeled
a bunch of fresh basil, chopped
250 ml/1 cup tomato juice
2 tablespoons olive oil, plus extra to serve
sea salt and freshly ground black pepper
a handful of ice, to serve
Tabasco or hot sauce, to serve

a food processor

serves 4–6

Prepare the tomatoes and cucumber by cutting them in half and removing the seeds with a teaspoon. Set the seeds aside, then finely dice the tomato and cucumber flesh and place in a mixing bowl. Dice the (bell) peppers and onion and add to the other vegetables along with the basil. Mix together.

Place about a third of your diced mixture into a food processor along with the reserved tomato and cucumber seeds, tomato juice and olive oil. Blend until smooth.

Pour the mixture over the remaining diced vegetables and mix together, adding salt and pepper to taste. Refrigerate until nicely chilled.

Serve in individual glasses with a drizzle of olive oil and an ice cube. Put some Tabasco sauce on the table for anyone who wants to add an extra kick.

Carpaccio of beef is one of those rare dishes that manages to satisfy the inner carnivore while still being seen as a light, diet-friendly choice. But despite its increasing popularity, it can make the squeamish break out into cold sweats. ('What, you mean completely raw?'.) One thing's for sure, though: this recipe is delicious and perfect as a summer starter.

Beef carpaccio with cherry tomato, basil & lemon dressing

- 250 g/9 oz. beef fillet (ask your butcher for a piece about 8–10 cm/ 3¼–4 inch thick)
- a good handful of cherry tomatoes
- a small bunch of fresh basil
- 100 ml/⅓ cup/ 6 tablespoons extra virgin olive oil
- ½ garlic clove, crushed
- freshly squeezed juice of 1 lemon
- a large handful of rocket/arugula
- sea salt and freshly ground black pepper
- Parmesan cheese, shaved, to serve
- a handful of pine nuts, toasted (optional), to serve

serves 4

Freeze the beef fillet for around 45 minutes. This will help make it far easier to slice, and while it's firming up you can prepare the dressing.

Cut the tomatoes into quarters and roughly chop or tear the basil. Mix them together with half the oil and the crushed garlic. Season with salt and pepper.

Mix the remaining olive oil with the lemon juice, adding a little extra salt and pepper to taste. The easiest way by far is to put them into an empty jam jar (or anything with a secure lid or top) and shake it like crazy. Alternatively, you could whisk the mix very quickly using a fork or small whisk. The secret here is to emulsify the two liquids so that they become one sauce rather than just droplets of lemon juice floating in oil.

Take the beef out of the freezer and slice it as thinly as possible. You should almost be able to see through the meat. If you're having difficulty getting it really thin, you can always put each slice between two pieces of clingfilm/plastic wrap and flatten them with a rolling pin.

To serve, lay the carpaccio slices on a serving platter, trying not to let them overlap too much. Scatter the tomato mixture, rocket/arugula and Parmesan shavings over the beef, along with a few good turns of the pepper mill. Give the lemon-oil emulsion another good stir or shake and drizzle it over the dish. You could also scatter pine nuts across the plate for extra bite.

A fantastically simple dish that hits all the right notes – smoky, succulent meat, lightened by the refreshing lemon and parsley combination, with breadcrumbs adding that bit of crunch. It's ideal barbecue food that can feed hundreds for next to no cost. It goes perfectly with a simple salad, or on a thick slice of grilled sourdough bread.

Grilled sardines with gremolata & toasted breadcrumbs

8 medium sardines, scaled and gutted
sea salt and freshly ground black pepper
lemon wedges, to serve
a handful of rocket/arugula leaves, to serve

For the breadcrumbs
2 thick slices of white sourdough bread
2 garlic cloves, bashed
a pinch of pine nuts
1 tablespoon extra virgin olive oil
a few sprigs of fresh rosemary, chopped
a few sprigs of fresh thyme, chopped

For the gremolata
a handful of fresh flat leaf parsley, roughly chopped
finely grated zest of 1 unwaxed lemon
1 garlic clove, finely grated
50 ml/scant ¼ cup/3 tablespoons extra virgin olive oil

a food processor
a grill pan or barbecue

serves 4

Start by preparing your breadcrumbs (it's a good idea to do these ahead of time so you can leave them to dry out and become extra crunchy). Tear the bread into pieces and put in a food processor. Blend until you have a rough, uneven consistency, then set aside. If in doubt, play it safe and keep the pieces big – the last thing you want is a fine powder that will turn into sludge when you try to toast it.

For the gremolata, mix together the parsley, lemon zest and garlic, add the oil and allow the flavours to infuse.

Pour a thin layer of oil over the base of a non-stick frying pan/skillet that's big enough to hold all the breadcrumbs comfortably in a single layer. Add the garlic cloves and set it over high heat. Remove the garlic once it begins to turn brown. Add the breadcrumbs, pine nuts and chopped herbs. Cook, stirring, so that the crumbs don't catch and burn. Once they have turned a lovely, crunchy golden brown, tip them out onto kitchen paper/paper towel and sprinkle generously with salt (this will help them dry out). You're done! They are pretty versatile and can be used as a form of seasoning for all kinds of dishes, such as grilled salmon, or on salads to add a bit of bite – whatever takes your fancy. They're also great mixed with grated Parmesan and loaded onto your favourite pasta.

Get your grill pan or barbecue heating to smoking hot. Season the sardines liberally with salt and gently place them on the grill horizontally. They shouldn't need any oil as there's enough in the skin already. They will take about 3–5 minutes on each side, depending on the heat. The secret to cooking fish on a grill is not to force it. If it's sticking and doesn't want to be turned, that's because it isn't ready to be turned, so leave it for another minute.

Scatter the fish with the gremolata and toasted breadcrumbs and serve with rocket/arugula and a wedge of lemon.

Squid are tricky little beasts that take posthumous revenge on inexperienced chefs by only allowing the tiniest window in which to cook them properly. Too little, and they'll have a gelatinous, outer-space feel to them. Too much, and you might as well go and chew on the sole of your shoe.

Chefs might wince at this, but as a general rule I recommend that squid only be grilled or deep-fried. I'm sure it's possible to pan-fry it perfectly, but I sure as hell can't do it. The secret when grilling squid is to weigh it down on the grill, otherwise it will curl up in an instant, which will inevitably lead to some parts being undercooked and others rubberized. Use the bottom of a frying pan/skillet or a heavy roasting pan.

Grilled squid with chorizo, feta & asparagus salad

1 bunch asparagus (about 8 stalks)
180 g/6⅓ oz. cooking chorizo, sliced
400 g/14 oz. squid (body and tentacles), cleaned
2 tablespoons olive oil
1 teaspoon hot paprika
100 g/3½ oz. feta cheese, crumbled
½ small bunch fresh flat leaf parsley, roughly chopped
100 g/3½ oz. rocket/arugula
sea salt and freshly ground black pepper
1 lemon, cut into wedges, to serve

a ridged grill pan

serves 4

Bring a pan of salted water to the boil. Remove the woody stems from the asparagus and cook for about 3–4 minutes, until they bend easily but will still snap if forced. Refresh under cold running water and cut each spear into three pieces.

In a separate pan, fry the chorizo for 5 minutes, until cooked through, then set aside and leave to cool.

Preheat the ridged grill pan until smoking hot. Slit open the squid tubes so that you have flat 'sheets' of squid. Gently score them with a sharp knife in a diamond pattern. Mix the paprika with a little olive oil and rub the mixture over the squid until it is completely covered. Season with salt and black pepper and place the squid flat on the hot grill, along with any tentacles. Put a frying pan/skillet or heavy roasting pan on top to stop the squid from curling up. Cook for about 1–2 minutes, depending on the thickness of your squid, then turn it over and cook for 1 more minute. Test a piece while it is cooking, just to be sure. It should offer just the slightest resistance to your bite. Remove from the pan and slice.

Combine the squid, asparagus, chorizo, feta, parsley and rocket/arugula on a plate, drizzle with a little olive oil and any cooking juices, and serve immediately with wedges of lemon.

Fish can often be a tough customer to pair up with other foods, and its delicate flavour is all too often swamped by what surrounds it. Not mackerel, though: it's in the heavyweight category, alongside red mullet and a few other choice bruisers. This recipe is a veritable slug-fest of flavours, each one vying for top spot with equal promise. Tarragon is one of the few herbs that seems to divide opinion, so feel free to swap it for basil if you're not a fan.

Grilled mackerel, orange, fennel & red onion salad with tapenade

8 large mackerel fillets
sea salt and freshly ground black pepper

For the salad
2 oranges
4 bulbs fennel
1 red onion
1 small bunch fresh flat leaf parsley, roughly chopped
1 sprig fresh tarragon or dill, roughly chopped

For the tapenade
250 g/9 oz. black olives (ideally Kalamata), pitted
1 garlic clove, peeled
30 g/¼ cup pine nuts
½ small bunch fresh basil
½ small bunch fresh flat leaf parsley
1 teaspoon dark navy rum
4 tablespoons olive oil
freshly squeezed juice of ½ lemon
3 tablespoons capers
3 anchovy fillets

For the vinaigrette
100 ml/⅓ cup olive oil
freshly squeezed juice of ½ lemon
a pinch of sugar

a ridged grill pan or barbecue

serves 6–8

For the tapenade, put all the ingredients in a food processor and pulse until amalgamated into a rough paste. Add a little extra oil to loosen it if the blades aren't catching everything. Set aside.

Meanwhile, prepare the oranges for the salad by cutting the skin off to reveal the flesh underneath. Using a sharp knife, carefully cut out each segment between the membranes so that you have a little wedge of pure orange with no white pith. You should end up with nice clean segments and a star-shaped central core of pith. Squeeze the central core to extract any juice and set aside to use in the vinaigrette). Slice the fennel and red onion as thinly as possible. Mix together the orange segments, fennel, red onion, parsley and tarragon.

Preheat the ridged grill pan or barbecue. Put all the vinaigrette ingredients, along with the reserved orange juice, in a jar and shake it to emulsify.

Season the mackerel fillets with salt and pepper, sprinkling a little extra on the skin side to help release the oils during cooking. Gently place them on the hot grill and cook for around 5 minutes, or until they can be turned over easily. Finish cooking on the other side.

Dress the salad with the vinaigrette and put the mackerel fillets on top. Spoon a little tapenade onto each fillet and serve.

I've always struggled with couscous salads. No matter what I did, the grains would always overcook and clump together. Then I was shown this technique by Pedro, our head chef. It's almost offensively easy, and produces perfect fluffy grains every time. To be honest, I'm not even sure it can be classified as cooking.

Fruit & nut couscous with fresh herbs

500 g/1 lb. 2 oz. couscous
olive oil, for frying and drizzling
50 g/⅓ cup whole almonds
50 g/⅓ cup whole cashews
50 g/½ cup whole pecans
1 pomegranate
2 tablespoons chopped fresh flat leaf parsley
2 tablespoons chopped fresh mint
2 tablespoons chopped fresh basil
50 g/¼ cup dried apricots, chopped
50 g/⅓ cup raisins
sea salt and freshly ground black pepper

serves 6–8

Put the couscous in a serving bowl and add cold water until it is covered by about 2 cm (¾ inch) water. Leave until all the water is absorbed (about 10 minutes), then fluff it up with your hands.

Put all the nuts in a pan with a splash of olive oil and toast over medium heat until they are nicely browned. Set aside to cool.

Remove the pomegranate seeds by cutting the fruit in half, holding it over a bowl and bashing the outside with the back of a wooden spoon so that the seeds fall into the bowl.

Stir the herbs, nuts, pomegranate seeds and dried apricots into the couscous. Add a little olive oil, season with salt and pepper and serve.

This flavourful salad is a regular favourite here at Megan's. It's vital that you use fresh breadcrumbs – pretty much any bread will do, though it's best to avoid ultra-heavy seeded breads. These have a tendency to break extremely expensive commercial food processors, so I dread to think what they'd do to a domestic variety!

The bread absorbs a lot of oil while frying, so it's important to use a good-quality extra virgin olive oil, and to remember that it isn't the lightest of salads, so go easy on the portions. You can make it go further by heaping it onto a bed of salad leaves. It also makes a great side with grilled fish.

Fried bread salad

250 g/9 oz. cooking chorizo
150 ml/⅔ cup extra virgin olive oil, plus extra for frying
4 garlic cloves, bashed
500 g/8⅓ cups fresh breadcrumbs
1 sprig fresh rosemary, finely chopped
200 g/7 oz. curly kale
1 x 400-g/14-oz. can cooked kidney beans, drained
sea salt
feta cheese, crumbled, to serve (optional)

a wok (optional)

serves 4–6

Remove the chorizo from its casing and roughly cut it into pieces. Heat a splash of olive oil in a frying pan/skillet, add the chorizo and fry over medium heat for 5 minutes until it has turned deep red. Allow to cool a little, then pulse in a food processor or chop very finely.

For best results, use a wok for the next part; its high sides will make frying the bread far easier. Put the oil and garlic in the wok or high-sided frying pan/skillet and heat over high heat for a few minutes, until the garlic begins to sizzle nicely. Continue to cook until golden brown all over, then remove and discard. Add the breadcrumbs and rosemary to the wok and fry, stirring regularly, until all the oil has been absorbed and the bread is golden and crunchy. Transfer to kitchen paper/paper towel (this helps to soak up some of the oil) and sprinkle with a little salt to draw out any excess moisture.

Bring a deep pan of salted water to the boil and add the kale. Cook for 4–5 minutes, then refresh under cold running water. The kale should retain a bit of bite.

Mix together the fried breadcrumbs, chorizo, kale and kidney beans, and serve. You can crumble some feta over the top if you like, but be careful it to adjust the seasoning so that it doesn't become too salty.

Crunchy fennel salad with pomegranate, mango & walnuts

Fennel is ubiquitous nowadays, as it rightfully should be. This is a great salad by itself, or as an accompaniment to grilled fish. Don't be scared to use the whole of the fennel – it adds colour to the dish. Reserve some of the sprightly leaves for decoration.

olive oil, for frying
50 g/½ cup walnuts
1 pomegranate
2 large or 4 small fennel bulbs, halved lengthwise and thinly sliced
1 small red onion, thinly sliced
1 firm mango, stoned/pitted and skinned, thinly sliced
1 red chilli, thinly sliced
1 tablespoon chopped fresh coriander/cilantro
1 teaspoon fresh lemon thyme leaves
freshly squeezed juice of 1 lime
sea salt and freshly ground black pepper

serves 4

Heat a splash of olive oil in a non-stick frying pan/skillet, add the walnuts and toast gently until golden brown. Once they're just right, remove from the pan and set aside. (If you leave them in, the residual heat will keep toasting them and before you know it you'll have blackened, bitter nuts.)

Remove the pomegranate seeds by cutting the fruit in half, holding it over a bowl and bashing the outside with the back of a wooden spoon so that the seeds fall into the bowl.

Mix all the ingredients together, season with salt and pepper and serve.

This is a great dish to prepare in advance when you have lots of guests, as it works perfectly served at room temperature. It's an amazingly easy marinade that also works wonders with fish, especially tuna and salmon.

Teriyaki chicken breast

4 skinless chicken breasts
olive oil, for frying
4 tablespoons soy sauce
2 teaspoons sesame oil
1 teaspoon fish sauce
2 tablespoons Thai sweet chilli sauce
1 teaspoon sesame seeds
2 tablespoons fresh coriander/cilantro leaves, chopped
1 red chilli, sliced
1 garlic clove, finely chopped
1 thumb-size piece fresh ginger, finely chopped
2 spring onions/scallions, sliced
salad leaves/greens or steamed pak choi/bok choy, to serve

a ridged grill pan
an ovenproof dish

serves 4

Preheat the oven to 220°C (425°F) Gas 7.

Ideally you'll need a ridged grill pan for this recipe. Don't fret if you don't have one – a regular non-stick frying pan/skillet will do just fine. Heat the pan until it is smoking hot. Rub a little olive oil onto the chicken breasts and cook for 3 minutes on each side, until the chicken is marked. Transfer to an ovenproof dish, cover with kitchen foil and cook in the preheated oven for a further 12 minutes, until cooked all the way through. Test the meat by pricking with a skewer and seeing whether the juices run clear. If they don't, just cook it for a little longer. Remove from the oven and leave to rest for 5 minutes, covered in kitchen foil to keep warm.

Meanwhile, gently warm a non-stick frying pan/skillet and toast the sesame seeds, stirring frequently, until golden brown, then remove from the pan to cool.

For the marinade, mix together all the remaining ingredients and add the toasted sesame seeds. Pour over the cooked chicken and leave to marinate for a few hours.

Serve with a crisp green salad or some steamed pak choi/bok choy.

A great-looking dish that's bound to get 'oohs' and 'aahs'. It tastes as good as it looks, and is totally foolproof. Don't worry if you don't have the time (or patience) to grill the nectarines – it's the combination of colours and flavours that makes this simple assembly dish such a hit.

Grilled nectarines with buffalo mozzarella, coppa salami & chilli

4 nectarines
caster/superfine sugar, for sprinkling
8 slices coppa salami (if you can't find any, substitute Parma ham)
250 g/9 oz. buffalo mozzarella, torn into generous hunks
1 mild red chilli, finely chopped (avoid the bird's eye variety, they're way too vicious for this dish)
a bunch of fresh basil leaves
3 tablespoons extra virgin olive oil
50 g/2 oz. Parmesan cheese, shaved
Reduced Balsamic Vinaigrette (see page 123), to serve
sea salt and cracked black pepper

a ridged grill pan

serves 4

Stone/pit the nectarines and cut them into quarters/fourths. Heat a ridged grill pan until smoking hot, sprinkle the nectarine pieces with sugar and cook for a few minutes on each side, until the char-lines show. Remove and allow to cool.

Mix together the nectarines, salami, mozzarella, chilli, basil and olive oil. Season with salt and black pepper.

Arrange on a plate, scatter with the shaved Parmesan and Reduced Balsamic Vinaigrette, and serve.

If I have one failing in the kitchen, it's a fetish for over-complicating things. Well, if truth be told I have quite a few failings in the kitchen (irritability, forgetfulness, a wanton disregard for pastry recipes... and I can't seem to make a cup of tea without a colander and six teaspoons ending up on the work surface. But I digress). I always want to throw in new ingredients, try a different method, do virtually anything other than sticking to the tried-and-tested recipe. Most of the time I succeed in making it slightly worse, but very occasionally I'll come up with something rather special, which I'll feel vindicates all my previous attempts. I'll eat it with a smug grin on my face, then promptly forget what I put in it.

This is one of those recipes that I've tried time and time again to improve, but have so far failed. It's just a handful of ingredients but it works so well that I very much doubt I'll ever better it. I'm going to keep trying, mind you. What's the point of cooking if you can't experiment?

Honey-roasted pear, crispy Parma ham & dolcelatte salad

4 pears (any type will do, but make sure they are fairly firm)
2 tablespoons clear honey
50 g/3½ tablespoons butter, melted
6 slices Parma ham
150 g/5 oz. dolcelatte cheese
150 g/5 oz. wild rocket/arugula
sea salt and freshly ground black pepper

serves 4

Preheat the oven to 200°C (400°F) Gas 6.

Core the pears and cut them into eight wedges lengthwise. Toss them with the honey and melted butter and season with salt and pepper. Bake them on a non-stick baking tray for about 15 minutes: you want them to have begun to turn golden and caramelized, but not to have lost their bite. This is why medium-to-firm pears are essential; if they are too ripe they will fall apart in the oven.

Place the Parma ham slices on a wire rack and roast in the oven for 8–10 minutes. Keep a vigilant watch over them, as they can go from pink to black faster than you think. They should be rigid and deeply coloured, but not burnt. Allow to cool on the rack.

Mix together the rocket/arugula, roasted pears and crispy ham. Scatter the dolcelatte over the salad as best you can – it's a sticky cheese, so it will resist being broken up. If you've had a bad day and can't be bothered with wrestling with an uncooperative dairy product, you can always opt for the more accommodating Roquefort or Stilton. The results are just as good.

Pearl barley, roast pumpkin & green bean salad

Pearl barley is great in salads, as it manages to retain a bit of texture and is one of the rare white ingredients, which makes it very useful for improving your salad aesthetics.

When it comes to green beans in salads, it is absolutely essential that they are cooked correctly. I still get school-canteen flashbacks whenever I see a limp, overcooked, or perhaps worst of all, sliced green bean. It's a traumatic experience that, once seen, can't be unseen. Don't subject anyone to it.

500 g/1 lb. 2 oz. pumpkin, peeled and cut into 3-cm/1¼-in cubes
200 g/generous 1 cup pearl barley
olive oil, for roasting
400 g/14 oz. green beans, topped but not tailed
100 g/3½ oz. sundried tomatoes, roughly chopped
20 pitted black olives
1 tablespoon capers
1 red onion, sliced
1 bunch fresh basil, roughly chopped
1 garlic clove, crushed
sea salt and freshly ground black pepper

serves 4–6

Preheat the oven to 200°C (400°F) Gas 6. Toss the pumpkin with a little olive oil and sea salt in a roasting pan. Roast for 20–25 minutes, until soft but not disintegrating.

In the meantime, bring a pan of salted water to the boil and cook the pearl barley for 20–30 minutes. It's impossible to give a precise cooking time, as each batch seems to be different (the same seems to apply to dried chickpeas, for some reason). You want the grains to be al dente, but not chalky or overly chewy. When they're ready, drain them and set aside.

For the beans, bring another pan of salted water to the boil and prepare a bowl of iced water. Add the beans and cook for 3–5 minutes. Test them by giving them a bend; you want them to be flexible but still have a nice snap if you push them too far. Once cooked, drain them and drop them immediately into the iced water. This 'refreshing' process will halt the cooking process and help keep the beans perfectly cooked and vibrantly green.

To assemble the salad, mix the pearl barley with the sundried tomatoes, olives, capers, red onion, basil and garlic. Add this to the roast pumpkin and green beans and stir gently until well combined. Drizzle with a little olive oil and serve.

the more the merrier

‘The kitchen is the heart of a home’ may be a cliché, but that doesn’t stop it from being true. Few memories have remained as vivid or as precious for me as the numerous family lunches my grandmother used to host in Italy. Countless cousins and uncles crammed together in the kitchen, gabbling away happily as they spooned steaming pasta onto each others’ plates. They may have been at each others’ throats just 10 minutes ago, but as soon as they were seated at the table all was forgotten (at least until after coffee). As a friend of mine once said, there’s nothing quite like war and food to bring people together.

Eating is a communal activity, the act of spooning peas onto your neighbour’s plate a silent confirmation of friendship. I’ve spent a lot of my life hosting dinners where I tried to prepare impressive cheffy food, making intricate dishes that I would arrange on each plate as if I was in a restaurant. Everyone made the standard coos of appreciation as the plate was placed in front of them, but it made the whole thing a bit, well, formal. I was so concerned with the food that I’d forgotten that the whole point is to have fun with your friends. Food is important, don’t get me wrong, but it should be a means of bringing people together. The best dinner parties I’ve been to have usually involved one of the guests tipsily cooking the appetizer with a glass of wine in their hand while another pops out to buy ice cream because the host’s infamous Chocolate Nemesis Cake has, once again, not even come close to setting (un-set chocolate cake makes a great sauce for ice cream, by the way!).

At Megan’s we’ve tried to bring a bit of that home-dining spirit to the restaurant world. Wherever possible, we offer dishes to share and encourage our customers to get involved with the serving. Our *côte de boeuf* arrives as a sizzling hunk of meat on the bone, served simply on an olive-wood board and partnered with a razor-sharp knife so that customers can carve it exactly as they like. When we host large parties we prepare huge banquet boards overflowing with salads, cured meats, bruschettas and oozing Camemberts. We lay them across the middle of a couple of trestle tables and everyone tucks in. It’s amazing how it brings everyone together.

The recipes in the section are not *haute cuisine*; they’re simple sharing fare to be enjoyed with as many friends as you can cram into your kitchen. Most are for 6–8 people, but can easily be increased.

I'm always amazed by how popular chicken liver pâté is, especially when you consider how fussy most people are when it comes to calf's liver. This is an adaptation of an old Tuscan recipe, commonly found on toasted bread as part of *antipasti misti*. It will keep in the fridge for a good few days once covered with oil.

Rustic chicken liver pâté with toasted baguette & cornichons

30 ml/2 tablespoons olive oil
1 red onion, diced
1 garlic clove, diced
500 g/1 lb. 2 oz. chicken livers
2 anchovy fillets, chopped
1 teaspoon chopped fresh thyme
2 tablespoons capers
2 tablespoons brandy
2 tablespoons chicken stock/broth
sea salt and freshly ground black pepper
baguette, sliced and toasted, to serve
cornichons and chutney, to serve

a food processor

serves 6–8

Heat a large pan over medium-low heat. Add the olive oil, onion and garlic. Cook for about 10 minutes, until the onion is soft and translucent. Increase the heat to medium high. Add the chicken livers, anchovies and thyme, along with a good amount of salt (liver needs bold seasoning). Cook for about 10 minutes, stirring frequently. The aim is keep the livers a little pink on the inside, as this will give your pâté a lovely, vibrant hue. Once cooked, remove the livers from the pan with a slotted spoon and set aside.

Add the capers, brandy and chicken stock to the pan. Bring to the boil and reduce by half. Place the chicken livers and cooking liquid in the bowl of a food processor and blitz quickly. We like a rougher, more rustic texture at the restaurant so we try to pulse it quickly, but you can blend it until smooth if you prefer. If the mixture seems too dry, just drizzle in a little olive oil while the blade is spinning until you achieve the desired consistency. Taste and add more seasoning if necessary. Serve with toasted baguette, cornichons and your favourite chutney.

Falafel with tzatziki

These are a far cry from those mouth-glue rocks that accompany your 4.00 a.m. kebab. The secret is the large amount of fresh coriander/cilantro and flat leaf parsley, which not only give the mixture fragrance and a brilliantly vibrant green colour, but also help keep it moist. They're best eaten as soon as they're fried and still gently warm on the inside. Leave them out too long, and the lovely crunchy exterior will go soft and spongy.

For the falafel
225 g/1 cup dried chickpeas
1 small red onion
3 garlic cloves
2 tablespoons ground coriander
2 tablespoons ground cumin
1 large bunch fresh coriander/cilantro
1 large bunch fresh flat leaf parsley
2 slices rustic white bread, crusts removed
4 tablespoons olive oil
vegetable oil, for frying
sea salt and freshly ground black pepper

For the tzatziki
1 cucumber
350 g/1½ cups natural thick Greek yogurt
freshly squeezed juice of ½ lemon
1 small bunch fresh mint, chopped
1 garlic clove, crushed
sea salt

a food processor
a deep-fat fryer

makes around 20–30

Give the chickpeas a quick rinse, then leave them to soak in plenty of water overnight.

Once soaked, put the chickpeas, along with all the other falafel ingredients except the vegetable oil, in a food processor and blend to a rough paste. Avoid the temptation of blending it too much; the falafel should still have texture when you bite into it.

Heat the vegetable oil to 180°C (350°F) in a deep-fat fryer. If you know what a quenelle is, well done you: take 2 dessertspoons and shape them like that. For the normal people out there, just take a scoop of the mixture and mould it into a rough ball shape with your hands. Fry the falafels in batches in the hot oil until they are very dark brown (they will colour quickly, but avoid the temptation to remove them from the oil. They need to fry for at least 3–4 minutes in order to crisp up properly). Remove and allow to cool on a wire rack.

For the tzatziki, cut the cucumber in half lengthwise. Use a teaspoon to scoop out the seeds and discard them. Grate the rest of the cucumber, then mix it with a little salt and leave in a colander to drain for 10 minutes (this helps remove the excess liquid, which would otherwise dilute your tzatziki). Stir the yogurt, lemon juice, mint and garlic into the cucumber. Season with extra salt if necessary, and serve with the falafel.

I can't quite explain why, but there's something about the look of this dish that really gets me going. The combination of creamy white mozzarella and robust, oily peperonata is a sight to behold. The only thing the combination lacks is crunch, which is where the ciabatta croutons come in. I sometimes break them up and scatter them over the whole of the dish, although you should only do that at the last minute or they'll get soggy.

Buffalo mozzarella with peperonata & rosemary ciabatta croutons

2 red (bell) peppers
2 yellow (bell) peppers
2 plum tomatoes
100 ml/⅓ cup/6 tablespoons olive oil
3 garlic cloves
1 red onion, sliced
2 bay leaves
1 tablespoon red wine vinegar
½ teaspoon salt
½ teaspoon sugar
1 tablespoon capers
a handful of cherry tomatoes, halved
a bunch of fresh basil
small ciabatta loaf
2 sprigs fresh rosemary, leaves finely chopped
4 balls buffalo mozzarella, approximately 150 g/ 5 oz. each, halved
sea salt and freshly ground black pepper
rocket/arugula leaves, to serve
a handful of toasted pine nuts, to serve

serves 6–8

The peperonata takes a while to cook and is (arguably) best served at room temperature, so I suggest making it in advance.

Quarter the (bell) peppers and remove the stalk, seeds and any of the white pith. Slice them into thin strips about 1 cm (½ inch) wide. Quarter the tomatoes, remove the seeds and chop them into small cubes.

Heat a deep frying pan/skillet over medium heat. Add the olive oil and garlic. Fry the garlic on both sides until golden brown, then remove from the pan and set aside. Add the red onion and cook, stirring frequently, until it is pale and translucent but not yet brown. Add the peppers, fried garlic and bay leaves. Cover and cook, covered, for 15 minutes or so, until the peppers are soft but still holding their shape.

Remove the lid and add the diced tomatoes, vinegar, salt and sugar. Cook, uncovered, for a further 10 minutes, then add the capers and cherry tomatoes and take off the heat. The residual heat in the peperonata will soften the cherry tomatoes, but not cook them to a mush. Leave to cool, then add the basil and season with salt and pepper if necessary.

For the rosemary ciabatta croutons, preheat the oven to 200°C (400°F) Gas 6. Slice the ciabatta on the diagonal as thinly as you can. Mix the rosemary with a little olive oil and brush it generously onto the ciabatta slices. You want the bread well coated in oil. Season with salt and bake on a wire rack for 5–8 minutes, until golden brown and crisp.

Serve the buffalo mozzarella on a bed of rocket/arugula and peperonata, with the ciabatta croutons and pine nuts scattered around.

This is a solid, chunky salad that can be prepared well in advance. Beware when cooking beetroot/beet, as everything in the vicinity ends up with red on it. It's as if the pan sneezes when you aren't looking.

Roasted butternut squash, beetroot & goats' cheese salad

- 4 raw beetroot/beets, ideally 2 red and 2 golden
- 50 ml/¼ cup clear honey
- 1 medium butternut squash, peeled, deseeded and cut into wedges
- olive oil, for roasting
- 2 sprigs fresh rosemary, chopped
- 200 g/7 oz. goats' cheese (the log variety works best here)
- ½ bunch fresh flat leaf parsley, chopped
- finely grated zest of 1 unwaxed lemon
- 50 g/⅔ cup flaked/sliced almonds
- sea salt and freshly ground black pepper
- baby spinach leaves or rocket/arugula, to serve

an ovenproof roasting pan, oiled

serves 4

Preheat the oven to 200°C (400°F) Gas 6.

Put the beetroot/beets into a pan with tepid water and bring to the boil. If you're using both the red and golden types, be sure to cook them separately or the gold colour will get cannibalized by the red. Cook them for approximately 45 minutes (I say approximately because the cooking time can vary wildly. We once had a pot on the stove for 5 hours and they still stubbornly refused to cook). Test them by inserting a knife; if the point goes in easily with little or no resistance, remove and drain in a colander. Run cold water over them and peel while still hot, as the skin comes off much more easily this way.

Cut the beetroot/beets into wedges and place them in the oiled roasting pan. Season generously with salt and pepper and drizzle with the honey.

In a separate roasting pan, mix the butternut squash with a splash of olive oil and the rosemary, and season with salt and pepper.

Put the beetroot/beets and butternut squash in the oven and roast for 45 minutes, or until golden brown. Remove and allow them to cool until you can handle them.

Remove the rind from the goats' cheese and crumble it. Mix the roasted vegetables with the parsley, goats' cheese, lemon zest and almonds. Serve on a bed of baby spinach or rocket/arugula.

This marinade works really well with all cuts of lamb. Shoulder is inexpensive and flavoursome, just be aware that it is quite fatty, so try and trim off as much excess as possible. If you want to play it safe, Barnsley chop or neck fillet are good alternatives.

Grilled Moroccan-spiced shoulder of lamb

1 butterflied shoulder of lamb, bone removed (approx. 1.6–2 kg/ 3½–4⅓ lbs. including bone)
2 tablespoons ground coriander
2 tablespoons ground cumin
2 tablespoons smoked paprika
1 tablespoon ground cinnamon
1 tablespoon garlic powder
2 tablespoons chopped fresh rosemary
olive oil, for the marinade
sea salt and freshly ground black pepper
1 quantity Tomato & Coriander/Cilantro Salsa (page 120), to serve

a barbecue

serves 4–6

This is so, so easy. Just mix all the herbs and spices together and loosen the mixture with olive oil. Baste it all over your lamb shoulder and leave it for at least 2 hours, or preferably overnight in the fridge. Remove it from the fridge and let it come to room temperature before you start to cook.

Get a barbecue seriously hot and place your lamb on the grill to cook. As the fat melts and renders, the barbecue will flare up and char the meat. If it's beginning to look a bit too black, spray a little water onto the coals to cool them. Cook for approximately 10 minutes on each side, then remove from the heat and leave to rest, covered with kitchen foil, for a further 10 minutes. Slice it into strips and serve with Tomato & Coriander Salsa. It also goes very well with tzatziki (see page 45).

Thai green curry is one of those dishes that seems to be loved by everyone. I have numerous friends who swear they're allergic to spicy food, but the allergy seems to miraculously subside when it's a green curry. Hmm… can't say I understand the logic there but I learned long ago that there's no use trying to argue against someone's food habits. Thankfully, this dish seems to be immune to most allergies and diet fads.

The trick of an authentic green curry is to get that typical Thai salty/sour tang by adding a large amount of Thai fish sauce and lime juice at the end. I've heard the urban legend of people making their own curry paste but I've never actually seen it happen. As long as you get a good-quality authentic paste, the results will be great. If the majority of the text on the packaging is in Thai, you're probably on the right track.

Thai green curry with toasted coconut rice

For the curry
2 tablespoons vegetable oil
3 shallots, sliced
3 sticks lemongrass, bashed
1 thumb-size piece of fresh ginger or galangal, peeled and chopped
2 garlic cloves, sliced
1 large bunch coriander/cilantro, with stalks, chopped
3 tablespoons Thai green curry paste
6 kaffir lime leaves
400 ml/1⅔ cups coconut milk
600 g/1 lb. 5 oz. chicken thigh fillets, cut into large chunks
300 g/11 oz. aubergine/eggplant, cut into 2.5-cm/1-inch cubes
1 teaspoon palm sugar
2 tablespoons lime juice
2 tablespoons Thai fish sauce
1 small bunch fresh basil (preferably Thai holy basil), chopped

For the rice
300 g/1½ cups basmati rice, rinsed a few times
50 g/⅔ cup desiccated coconut
½ fresh coconut, coarsely grated
2 spring onions/scallions, thinly sliced

serves 4–6

Heat the oil in a heavy-based pan over medium-high heat and add the shallots. Fry for 2 minutes, then add the lemongrass, ginger, garlic and chopped coriander/cilantro stalks (keep the leaves for later). Fry for a further 2 minutes, then add the curry paste and lime leaves. Stir well to combine.

Once the curry paste is beginning to bubble and spit, add the coconut milk. Bring to the boil, then reduce the heat to a simmer and add the chicken and aubergine/eggplant. Simmer for about 10 minutes, or until the chicken is cooked through.

Remove from the heat and add the palm sugar, lime juice, fish sauce, chopped coriander/cilantro leaves and basil. Check the seasoning and add more fish sauce if you feel it doesn't have enough salt.

For the rice, bring a pan of salted water to the boil, add the rice and cook for 15 minutes, then drain and leave to steam for 5 more minutes. In the meantime, heat a frying pan/skillet over medium heat and toast the desiccated coconut until it turns golden brown. Stir the toasted coconut, grated fresh coconut and spring onions/scallions into the rice and serve with the green curry.

Lamb shank tagine with lemon & parsley couscous

One of those dishes that fills your house with a warm, inviting fragrance. Choose your shanks wisely, as some can be huge and any waist-watching diners will quiver at the sight of them.

This will keep perfectly in the fridge for a good few days, but be aware that it's a nightmare to reheat as the shanks are so unwieldy. My advice is to prepare it the night before and leave it the pot with a lid on in the refrigerator, ready to be reheated when you need it. Of course, if we did that at the restaurant the Food Safety Officer would beat me around the head with a spatula, but what you do in your own home is up to you, and it's by far the easiest way.

1 large bunch fresh coriander/cilantro
2 garlic cloves
2 tablespoons paprika
2 tablespoons ground cumin
1 tablespoon ground coriander
grated zest of 1 unwaxed lemon
flour, for dusting
4 lamb shanks
olive oil, for frying
1 red onion, chopped
1 green (bell) pepper, cut into strips
1 litre/4 cups tomato juice
20 cherry tomatoes
sea salt and freshly ground black pepper
1 quantity Fruit & Nut Couscous (page 25), to serve

Put the fresh coriander/cilantro (the whole bunch, stalks and all), garlic, paprika, cumin, ground coriander and lemon zest in the blender and pulse until it is all mixed together.

Season the flour with a little salt and pepper and toss the lamb shanks in it until coated. Heat a heavy-based casserole dish over high heat, add a little olive oil and brown the meat on all sides until nicely golden. Remove and set aside.

Add a little more oil, if needed, and the red onion and green (bell) pepper. Fry gently for about 10 minutes, until the onion has softened and is beginning to caramelize. Add the spice paste and fry for a further 10 minutes, stirring frequently. Add the lamb shanks and tomato juice and bring to the boil. Reduce the heat to its lowest setting and simmer for 1½–2 hours. The meat should be very tender, but should not have fallen off the bone completely. About 10 minutes before the end of the cooking time, add the cherry tomatoes so that they can soften a little.

Best served with couscous, such as Fruit & Nut Couscous (see page 25).

Fish pie

For the poaching liquor
1 bunch fresh flat leaf parsley
600 ml/2½ cups whole/full-fat milk
1 white onion, sliced
2 cloves
4 garlic cloves
4 black peppercorns
2 sprigs fresh rosemary
2 sprigs fresh thyme
2 bay leaves
250 g/9 oz. smoked haddock, cut into chunks

For the filling
4 eggs
200 g/7 oz. cod fillet, cut into chunks
100 g/3½ oz. raw king prawns/jumbo shrimp, shelled
50 g/2 oz. frozen peas

For the white sauce
50 g/3½ tablespoons butter
50 g/generous ⅓ cup plain/all-purpose flour

For the topping
1 kg/2¼ lbs. potatoes
100 g/3½ oz./7 tablespoons butter
100 ml/⅓ cup double/heavy cream
sea salt and freshly ground black pepper

a piping/pastry bag (optional)

serves 4–6

Preheat the oven to 185°C (365°F) Gas 4–5.

Separate the parsley leaves from the stalks and set the leaves aside for later. Put the parsley stalks and the rest of the poaching liquor ingredients, except the haddock, in a large, wide pan and heat over medium heat until hot but not boiling (you don't want to boil the milk). Reduce the heat to a gentle simmer, add the haddock and cook for about 8 minutes. Remove the haddock and set aside. Strain the poaching milk through a sieve/strainer and reserve the liquor for later.

Bring a small pan of water to the boil and gently lower in the eggs one by one (if you drop them in you risk cracking them). Cook them for 8 minutes, then remove and cool under running water. Peel and cut into wedges.

Prepare the topping by peeling the potatoes and cutting them into 5-cm (2-inch) chunks. Put them in a deep pan and cover with ample cold water and a good pinch of salt. Bring it to the boil, then reduce the heat and simmer until tender (you can test this by inserting a knife into one of them; if it passes through with very little resistance, it's cooked). Drain in a colander and return to the pan. If you have a vegetable mouli, pass the potatoes through it. If not, mash them with a potato ricer or hand masher. Put the butter and double/heavy cream in a small pan and warm gently until the butter has melted, then add to the cooked potatoes and stir until fully absorbed. You want the mash to be creamy and pliable, so add a little more cream if necessary. Season with salt and pepper.

Now it's time to make the white sauce (I know, it's all a bit laborious but you can prepare the pie well in advance, so give yourself ample time and don't rush). In a medium pan, melt the butter over medium heat. Add the flour and stir well. This is known as the roux. Keep cooking it for a minute or two, stirring constantly, to get rid of any floury taste. Add a ladle of the poaching liquor and stir until it has all been incorporated. Continue doing this until all the liquor has been added. The sauce should have a coating consistency: in other words, if you dip a wooden spoon into it and draw a horizontal line with your finger across the spoon, the line you've drawn should remain there. If it's too thin, keep cooking it over a low heat until it has thickened. Taste and season with salt and pepper if necessary.

Chop the reserved parsley leaves. Add the haddock, cod, king prawns/jumbo shrimp, frozen peas, parsley and boiled egg wedges to the white sauce, then pour into an ovenproof dish. Using a piping/pastry bag (if available), pipe the mashed potato onto the pie, trying to make sure that there is a good seal around the edges of the dish so that nothing leaks out during cooking. If you don't have one, spoon the potato onto the fish.

Bake in the oven for 25 minutes. If the potato peaks are not looking enticingly brown, put it under the grill/broiler for a few minutes.

Take a bow and enjoy!

There are countless fish pie recipes knocking around, and this one isn't reinventing the wheel, so don't expect a pan-Asian twist or a lactose-free version. This is a classic, dozy-making, third-helping-is-a-necessity fish pie. The trick is to give the milk as much flavour as possible, which we achieve by cooking the smoked haddock in it first with lots of herbs. As well as the smoked haddock, you can use any fish you like.

I had always wondered why ragùs in Italy are so different from the ubiquitous, sloppy Spag Bol you find in other places. Surely it's just a question of slow-cooking some meat with a few vegetables? In essence it is, but four tricks make all the difference. First, a paste-like vegetable base. Second, chicken livers (you won't notice them, but they add a deep savouriness to the sauce). Third, a very long cooking time. Fourth, as with all good Italian cooking, an industrial quantity of olive oil. It's best made a day in advance.

Pappardelle with traditional ragù

3 red onions
3 sticks celery
3 carrots
4 garlic cloves
1 small bunch fresh flat leaf parsley
1 small bunch fresh basil
125 ml/½ cup olive oil (or more if you like)
200 g/7 oz. chicken livers, finely chopped
200 g/7 oz. minced/ground pork
800 g/1¾ lbs. minced/ground beef
350 ml/1½ cups red wine
500 ml/2 cups beef stock/broth
1 tablespoon tomato concentrate
800 g/1¾ lbs. canned chopped tomatoes
2 bay leaves
2 sprigs fresh rosemary
750 g/1⅔ lbs. pappardelle
75 g/3 oz. Parmesan cheese, grated
sea salt and freshly ground black pepper
shaved Parmesan and fresh basil leaves, to serve

a food processor

serves 6–8

Very roughly chop the onion, celery, carrots, garlic, parsley and basil. Put them in a food processor and pulse until very finely chopped, almost a paste. You could do this by hand, but it will be a painstaking task. Don't be tempted to skip this and just chop them roughly. The idea is to have a viscous, rich sauce, not a watery slop with a chunk of onion here and a slice of celery there.

In a heavy-based casserole dish, heat the olive oil over a medium-high heat and fry your vegetable mixture, stirring frequently. Add a little more oil if it looks too dry. After 10 minutes, add the chicken livers and cook for a further 5 minutes. Add the pork and beef, stir well, then add the red wine. Increase the heat and cook for 5 minutes. Add the beef stock/broth, tomato concentrate, chopped tomatoes, bay leaves and rosemary. Bring to the boil, then reduce the heat to its lowest setting and cover, leaving just the tiniest of gaps for the steam to escape. Simmer for at least 3 hours, ideally 4, adding a little water along the way if the sauce has dried out. Remember to stir it every now and then, paying particular attention that nothing catches and burns on the base of pan. The end result should be an intense, dark-coloured ragù with a little oil floating on top.

To finish the dish, bring a pan of water to the boil. Add a pinch of salt and cook the pasta, following the instructions on the packet. Reheat the sauce, if necessary. Drain the pasta and mix with the sauce and grated Parmesan. Scatter with shaved Parmesan and a few torn basil leaves and serve.

Thanksgiving roast pumpkin stuffed with sweet potato mash & marshmallows

My closest friends are a family of three brothers who grew up in New York during the first years of their lives. Despite being London based for the last 20-odd years, they still avidly maintain the tradition of a yearly Thanksgiving dinner. They provide the roast bird, which is all too often a macabre combination of a chicken stuffed in a duck stuffed in a turkey, imaginatively named 'turducken' (don't try asking for this in London's more reputable and old-fashioned butchers; they'll adopt a Jeeves-like air of superiority and snootily point out that 'what you mean, surely, is "bird-in-bird", Sir.')

Every year I'm asked to prepare this dish, a rich, sticky combination that sounds odd but in fact works amazingly. I've often wondered whether it could be served as a dessert, but I confess I've never tried.

- 1 small pumpkin, about 15 cm/6 inch across
- olive oil, for roasting
- 4 large sweet potatoes, cut into equal chunks
- 1 cinnamon stick
- 2 cloves
- 50 g/3½ tablespoons butter
- 75 ml/scant ⅓ cup double/heavy cream
- 1 teaspoon ground cinnamon
- ¼ teaspoon ground nutmeg
- ¼ teaspoon ground ginger
- 1 teaspoon caster/granulated sugar
- 1 teaspoon clear honey, plus extra for drizzling
- 30 g/1 oz. mini marshmallows
- 30 g/1 oz. pecans
- sea salt, to taste

serves 4 as a side for a roast dinner

Preheat the oven to 220°C (425°F) Gas 7. Cut the top off the pumpkin and discard it. Using a sturdy spoon, scoop out all the seeds and pith from the centre and discard them. Drizzle a little olive oil and salt into the pumpkin and roast for around 40 minutes, or until it is lightly browned at the edges and the inside is cooked through. Be careful when you open the oven, as you'll get a faceful of scalding steam for your trouble. Once cooked, remove and set aside.

While the pumpkin is cooking, put the sweet potatoes in a pan and cover with tepid water. Add the cloves, cinnamon sticks and a pinch of salt. Bring to the boil and cook, uncovered, for about 30 minutes, until a knife passes through them with little or no resistance. Drain in a colander, remove the cinnamon stick and cloves and return to the pan. Add the butter, cream, sugar, ground cinnamon, nutmeg and ginger. Mash with a potato masher. It won't be easy to get a totally smooth consistency, but do your best. Add the honey and season with salt to taste.

Spoon the sweet potato mash into the hollowed-out pumpkin and top with the pecans, mini marshmallows and a little drizzle of honey. The residual heat of the mash should be enough to melt the marshmallows, but you can always pop it in the oven for 5 more minutes if necessary. Serve!

Roast pork belly with apple, leek & fennel two ways

I went to a restaurant the other day, a good one, and ordered belly/side of pork. What arrived was meltingly soft, flavoursome pork meat topped by a soggy, flabby piece of skin. What the hell? I don't normally get het up or make a fuss in restaurants but really, a roast belly of pork with soft skin? The main reason – in fact the only reason – I ever order it is so that I can grin like a two-year old while I tap-tap-tap away at the rock hard, salty crackling.

I still ate it, of course, because I'm a glutton, but I did so with an indignant sneer. If your belly/side of pork has a soft skin, go and stand in the corner and hang your head in shame. You're no friend of mine.

For the pork & roasted vegetables

1.3–1.5 kg/2¾–3¼ lbs. pork belly/side
table salt, for rubbing the pork
3 apples, cored and cut into eighths
2 leeks, cut into 3-cm/1¼-inch rings
2 white onions, cut into eighths
1 bulb fennel, cut into eighths
10 garlic cloves, skin on
a small bunch of fresh thyme

For the salad

1 leek, halved lengthwise and very thinly sliced
3 apples, cored and thinly sliced
1 bulb fennel, thinly sliced
1 tablespoon chopped fresh mint
1 tablespoon chopped fresh flat leaf parsley

For the dressing

100 ml/⅓ cup olive oil
1 tablespoon Dijon mustard
1 tablespoon clear honey
freshly squeezed juice of 1 lemon
sea salt and freshly ground black pepper

a very sharp knife

serves 6

Preheat your oven as hot as it will go.

Using a very sharp knife, carefully score the skin of the belly/side, making cuts about 2.5 cm (1 inch) apart and taking care to cut through the skin and fat but stopping before you hit the meat. Rub table salt all over the skin, making sure you get it into the scores. The salt will draw out the water during cooking and will help crisp up the skin. Season the underside of the pork, but less generously.

Put the pork in a deep roasting pan and roast for 30 minutes. Don't open the oven every 2 minutes to check it, or all the heat will escape. Carefully remove the pork and reduce the oven temperature to 180°C (350°F) Gas 4. Lift the pork out of the pan and set it aside for a minute. Add the apples, leeks, onions, fennel, garlic and thyme to the pan and sit the pork back on top. Return the pan to the oven and cook for another hour. If the skin is looking too crispy (apparently that's possible), cover it with kitchen foil.

While the pork is cooking, prepare all the salad ingredients. Put the salad dressing ingredients together in an empty jar, close and shake until combined. Toss the salad with the dressing.

Serve generous hunks of pork with the roasted vegetables and the salad. Apple chutney also goes down a treat with this.

I admit, we don't serve this at Megan's, much as I'd like to. It was actually the result of a dinner-party crisis I once had, when my lovingly prepared home-made vanilla ice cream decided to melt during a car journey, forcing me to knock up an alternative with whatever I had at hand. In fairness, I probably should have seen it coming, considering it was a 4-hour drive in the height of summer, but let's not get bogged down in the detail. This is what I came up with.

Cheat's blood orange & amaretto ice cream

5 blood oranges
4 tablespoons caster/ granulated sugar
250 g/9 oz. amaretti biscuits
50 ml/scant ¼ cup amaretto liqueur
500 ml/1 pint/2 cups good-quality vanilla ice cream

serves 4

Start by making a blood orange coulis, which will then be stirred into the ice cream. Zest the darkest of the blood oranges and juice all of them. You need around 250 ml (1 cup) juice. Combine the juice and sugar in a pan and cook over medium heat, stirring, until all the sugar has melted. Continue simmering to reduce the liquid until you have a thin syrup, then add the zest and remove from the pan and allow to cool. It will thicken up impressively as it cools. You can test this by removing a teaspoonful while it's cooking and spreading it on a cold side plate. This will give you a good idea of what you'll end up with once the syrup cools.

Put the amaretti biscuits in a separate bowl and crush them with your hands until they are nicely broken up into approximately 1-cm (½-inch) chunks. Don't get over-excited, as they're useless once they become too small. Put the chunks in a colander and give it a gentle shake to get rid of any powdered crumbs.

Set aside about a third of the amaretti chunks for later. Douse the rest with the amaretto liqueur and stir gently so that it all gets soaked up.

Take the ice cream out of the freezer and tip it into a mixing bowl. What we're aiming to do is let it soften to the point that ingredients can be stirred in, but not to let it go so far that it melts completely. Keep a careful eye on it, since once it's melted fully you can't rescue it by putting it back in the freezer, as it will separate and form layers.

Once you can work the ice cream easily with a wooden spoon, pour in the macerated amaretti chunks and mix until incorporated. Add the blood orange syrup and dry amaretti chunks and stir gently until they are distributed evenly. Ideally you want the syrup to give the ice cream streaks, rather than turning it all a uniform shade of pink.

Place in the freezer to firm up, then serve.

Summer fruit pavlova

Meringues by themselves can be dry, cloying affairs, better to look at than to eat (and once they get stuck in your teeth they won't budge for love nor money). A pavlova, on the other hand, is the definition of a balanced dessert. Unctuous but with a solid crunch, sweet but balanced by the fruit's acidity, when well decorated it is a majestic sight to behold. It will collapse into a gory mess as soon as you start serving, though, so get the photos in first.

For the pavlova base
5 egg whites
300 g/1½ cups plus 1 tablespoon caster/ granulated sugar
1 teaspoon cornflour/ cornstarch
1 teaspoon vanilla extract/ vanilla bean paste

For the filling
350 ml/3½ cups double/ heavy cream
1½ tablespoons icing/ confectioners' sugar
strawberries, blackberries, raspberries, passion fruit, redcurrants and kiwis, to serve

a piping/pastry bag (optional)
an electric whisk or balloon whisk
a baking sheet lined with baking parchment

serves 8

Preheat the oven to 120°C (250°F) Gas 1.

The pavlova base needs to cook overnight, so plan this one in advance. Once cooked, it will happily last for a week in dry conditions. If you're looking to impress, you'll need a piping/pastry bag so that you can give the meringue shape, but don't worry if you don't have one, the rustic look is also very much in vogue.

Combine the egg whites and caster/granulated sugar in a large mixing bowl. Using an electric whisk (easy) or a balloon whisk (exhausting), whisk them to medium peaks. In other words, when you lift the whisk out, you should have peaks that stand under their own weight, but the very tops will be a little limp-wristed. Add the cornflour/ cornstarch and vanilla extract/vanilla bean paste and gently fold them in.

Put the meringue mixture in a piping/pastry bag and pipe or spoon it out in whatever style you like onto the prepared baking sheet – just make sure that it is vaguely round and not too thin. Bake for 1½ hours, then turn off the oven and leave the meringue inside overnight. Don't open the oven door at any point or the heat will escape.

Using a serrated knife, cut the top off the pavlova, reserving it to stir into yoghurt with some jam for tomorrow's breakfast. Pour the cream into a mixing bowl along with the icing/confectioners' sugar. Whisk to stiff peaks. Spoon or pipe the cream into the centre of the meringue and decorate with fruit to your heart's content.

One of our most popular desserts, you can see people's eyes widen as we bring this out. Don't let the healthy-sounding gluten-free label fool you – these are dense bricks of gooey chocolate. Avoid talking while eating, it isn't an attractive sight.

Gluten-free chocolate brownie tower

30 g/¼ cup rice flour
30 g/¼ cup cocoa powder
125 g/4¼ oz. dark chocolate
125 g/4¼ oz./1 stick plus 1 tablespoon butter
3 eggs
250 g/1¼ cups caster/superfine sugar

For the decoration
250 ml/1 cup double/heavy cream
icing/confectioners' sugar, to taste
summer fruits, such as strawberries, blackberries, raspberries and redcurrants (whatever you can get your hands on), to serve

a brownie pan, greased and lined with baking parchment
an electric whisk (optional)
a piping/pastry bag (optional)

serves 6–8

Preheat the oven to 180°C (350°F) Gas 4.

Start by preparing the brownie pan. The butter will act as an adhesive and should hold the paper in place. It helps if you cut a shape that is bigger than your pan and then make a cut at each corner: that way the paper can sit tight in the corners and give you the best fit.

Start by passing the rice flour and cocoa powder through a fine sieve/strainer to get rid of any lumps. Melt the butter and chocolate together. You can do this the traditional way over a bain-marie (place them in a heatproof bowl set over a pan of barely simmering water, making sure the bottom of the bowl isn't touching the water). Personally I can never see the point when a microwave is just as effective! Just put them in a plastic bowl and melt on a medium setting. Once the butter and chocolate have melted, give them a gentle stir until they are fully combined. Don't over-stir, or the chocolate will become grainy.

In a separate bowl, beat the eggs with the caster/granulated sugar until all the sugar has been incorporated and you have a pale yellow paste. It helps if you have an electric whisk, but it can also be done by hand.

Add the flour and cocoa powder to the egg mixture and fold it in, then add the melted chocolate and butter mixture and fold it in.

Pour the mixture into the prepared pan, then drop it onto your work surface a couple of times to get rid of any bubbles (this helps to make an extra-rich, gooey brownie). Bake in the oven for 30 minutes, then leave it to cool in the pan. Don't worry if the top has cracked a little, it's fine.

Cut into squares, then stack them randomly on a serving dish, one on top of another, as high as you dare.

Whip the cream with some icing/confectioners' sugar (the quantity depends entirely on how sweet you like it). If you have a piping/pastry bag, fill it with the cream and pipe it over the tower; if not, just spoon it over. Dot the tower with the summer fruits, dust with a little icing/confectioners' sugar and serve.

We have my shoddy business acumen to thank for this recipe. It was my first Christmas at the restaurant and I was a little over-excited after 28 years of being force-fed capitalism's dubious take on the birth of a religious figure. I was convinced that whatever Christmas-related products I offered in the shop would be snapped up by a wide-eyed public delirious on the heady mix of gaudy lights, forced altruism and daytime drinking, so in my infinite wisdom I bought 50 panettones on the cusp of one of the worst recessions in living memory. This is where they ended up.

Panettone crème caramel

250 g/1⅓ cups caster/superfine sugar, plus 400 g/2 cups for the caramel
6 eggs
200 ml/¾ cups whole/full-fat milk
1 small 300-g/10-oz. panettone, sliced

an ovenproof, watertight mould, or individual moulds

serves 6–8

A basic crème caramel mixture is simply equal volumes of milk, sugar and eggs mixed together. How much you'll need depends entirely on how big or small you want it to be! We normally use an 8-cm (3¼-inch) circular ring-shaped mould, which requires about 6 eggs and the quantities given here. You can use whatever you like, provided it is ovenproof and watertight (you'll need to cook the dish in a bain-marie), adjusting the quantities and cooking time as necessary.

Preheat the oven to 170°C (340°F) Gas 3½.

Start by making the caramel. Pour a thin layer of sugar into a dry, flat frying pan/skillet. Warm over medium heat until the sugar starts to dissolve into a caramel. Give the sugar a swirl every now and then but don't stir at all. Once all the sugar has dissolved, continue cooking for 30 seconds more until the caramel has gone a shade darker, then quickly and carefully pour it into your mould. Be careful: the worst burns I've seen in kitchens have been caused by caramel. Leave it to cool in the dish.

Put the kettle on for the bain-marie. Mix together equal volumes of eggs, sugar and milk in a bowl. Dip the panettone slices into the mixture until they are saturated, and place them on top of the caramel until you have a complete layer. Repeat with a second layer, then pour the remaining mixture on top, until the dish is full. Place the dish in a deep roasting pan and pour boiling water around the dish until it comes up to about three-quarters of the height of your mould. Cover it very loosely with kitchen foil and bake in the oven for approximately 25 minutes. You can check to see if it's ready by shaking the dish gently; if it is still liquid in the centre, bake it for a further 5 minutes.

Once cooked, remove it from the bain-marie and leave to cool. Run a knife around the outside of the caramel to loosen it from the dish, then turn it onto a serving dish.

I don't usually opt for dessert when I'm dining out. I would if I could, but after the shirt-popping amount of first and main course I consume, I just can't bring myself to tackle a third course. I'll scan the dessert menu just because I'm too full to argue. Brownie? No. Sorbet? No. Plum Cobbler? God no! There's only one sweet which will spur me on regardless, and that's banoffee. I just can't resist.

This recipes calls for two cans of condensed milk, as I find the caramel the best bit, but if you want to go lighter, just use one. My recommendation is to use two and then keep some left over to spoon onto ice cream another day.

Banoffee pie

2 x 397-g/14-oz. cans condensed milk
350 g/12 oz. biscuits/cookies, ideally a nice oaty type with a bit of texture (we use Hob Nobs)
100 g/3½ oz/7 tablespoons butter, melted
400 ml/1⅔ cups double/heavy cream
3 bananas, sliced
150 g/5 oz. milk/semisweet chocolate, grated
toasted flaked/sliced almonds, to serve (optional)

a 24 cm/9 inch springform cake pan
a food processor (optional)

serves 8–10

Start by making the caramel, as it takes quite some time. This is one of the culinary world's most miraculous and effortless achievements. Place the can(s) of condensed milk, unopened, in a pan and cover with cold water. Make sure they are completely submerged. Bring to the boil and simmer for 1¾ hours, topping up the water if it no longer covers the tops of the cans. Remove and leave to cool before opening.

Crush the biscuits/cookies by pulsing them in a food processor or putting them in a plastic bag and bashing them. Don't get too carried away; you want them to look like fresh breadcrumbs, not sawdust. Mix them with the melted butter and press them into the cake pan, covering both the base and the sides. Put it in the fridge to harden for 20 minutes.

Meanwhile, whip the cream until it stands up on its own.

Spoon the cooled caramel over the biscuit base, then layer the bananas on top. Spread the whipped cream over the bananas and top with grated chocolate and almonds, if using. Serve immediately.

two's company

As much as I'm a fan of large dinners with all and sundry, there is something special about a dinner for two. It is an intimate act, and I don't just mean in a romantic sense. It's irreducibly private. The public's eyes and ears can go almost anywhere nowadays, but somehow a *tête-à-tête* dinner is still sacrosanct. The press can take photos of topless celebrities all they want, but recording a private conversation over dinner? Come on, we do have standards, you know…

When you sit face-to-face with someone over a meal you have all their attention, and they have all yours. There's no dodging the topic or breaking away, and you will know your guest well by the time dessert rolls around, although whether you like them or not is entirely another matter. I'm relatively easy to please; provided you're happy for me to drink a glass more than I should, and have the patience to listen to me rant about the Finnish Winter War, we'll get along perfectly. Just don't use the expressions 'it's for the best' or 'aww, bless!' unless you want your panna cotta on the floor.

I'm making a big deal about the social intimacy of a dinner for two, but don't for a second think that the food isn't important. It's the glue, the lynchpin that allows the whole conversational cog to turn. I'm not sure how you'd react, but if someone invited me over for 'a nice long chat over an empty table', I'd run a mile. Food is the whole reason for the event, and as such it deserves special attention. A dinner prepared with love and care acts as a testament to how much you value your guest; the effort will be appreciated, I guarantee it.

Cooking for two lets you really push the culinary boat out, dedicating time, effort and expense that is prohibitive when cooking for more people. It's not an occasion for rushing; you can savour every bite of food and every morsel of conversation, so get the pans out, light the candle, and stick two fingers up to yet another TV dinner. This is a special occasion!

Whole baked Camembert

This is one of the most popular starters on the menu, and one of the easiest to replicate at home. We serve it as part of our large antipasti platters along with chutney and toasted bread. As a romantic sharing starter, you can't go wrong with this (unless your guest is lactose intolerant, in which case you're going very wrong, but serves you right for not doing your homework).

1 x 250-g/9-oz. Camembert, in its wooden box
1 garlic clove, cut into 4 strips lengthwise
a sprig of fresh thyme, leaves stripped then chopped
olive oil, to drizzle
baguette, sliced and toasted, to serve

serves 2 as a starter/appetizer

Preheat the grill/broiler to its highest setting.

Remove any plastic or paper wrapping from the Camembert and put it back in its box.

Make an X-shaped cut in the top of the Camembert and insert the strips of garlic. Sprinkle the thyme leaves on top and drizzle with a little olive oil.

Put the Camembert in the microwave for 1 minute on its highest setting, then remove and place under the grill/broiler for about 5 minutes, until deep brown and bubbling on top. Serve immediately.

Roasted figs with Parma ham, Gorgonzola & honey

The Italians have long been advocates of pairing fruit with cheese. I can still remember my mother earnestly telling me *al contadino non far sapere quant'è buono il cacio con le pere* ('don't tell the farmer how good pecorino is with pears'). Why she had it in for the poor farmer is anybody's guess, but she was right, it's an amazing combination.

This recipe shows off another stunning pairing of fruit and cheese, the crispy Parma ham acting as a corset that holds the little bundle together. The secret is to find figs that have just become ripe. Too early and they taste of nothing, too late and they disintegrate in the oven. You can double the quantities (as pictured) for larger groups or you might just need more for hungry couples.

4 black or green figs, (whichever you prefer)
125 g/4½ oz. Gorgonzola cheese
4 thin slices Parma ham
1 tablespoon runny honey
Reduced Balsamic Vinaigrette (see page 123)

a baking sheet, lined with baking parchment

serves 2 as a starter/appetizer

Preheat the oven to 200°C (400°F) Gas 6.

Cut a cross into the top of the figs, cutting until you're about half way down. Squeeze the base of the figs so that they open like flowers.

Stuff some Gorgonzola into each fig, and wrap each fig with slice of Parma ham around the middle. You can use a toothpick to hold it in place if necessary.

Arrange the figs on the prepared baking sheet, making sure they have plenty of space between them for the heat to circulate and allow the ham to crisp up (there's nothing worse than soggy, steamed Parma ham).

Drizzle honey liberally over the figs, making sure you get some in the cavity.

Roast in the oven for 6–8 minutes, until the Parma ham is crispy and the cheese has melted.

Serve two baked figs per person, spooning over a few drops of Reduced Balsamic Vinaigrette and any leftover cooking juices.

Bruschetta of caponata & marinated mozzarella

Caponata is one of the gutsiest, most robust dishes I know. An old Sicilian favourite, it can go round for round with the meatiest of stews. It keeps well, so it's worth making an extra-large batch. It generally tastes best when served at room temperature.

The marinated mozzarella is a dish unto itself, and a cheat's way of making ordinary mozzarella taste like creamy burrata. Scattered with some cherry tomatoes and a little homemade pesto, it becomes a perfect summer appetizer. In this recipe, the soft unctuousness balances perfectly with the in-your-face caponata.

2 thick slices sourdough bread
1 garlic clove, halved
sea salt and freshly ground black pepper

For the marinated mozzarella
125 g/4½ oz. mozzarella balls
2 tablespoons crème fraîche
1 tablespoon double/heavy cream
1 tablespoon olive oil
grated zest of ½ unwaxed lemon
5 large, fresh basil leaves, finely chopped, plus extra whole leaves, to serve

For the caponata
vegetable oil, for frying
2 large aubergines/eggplants, cubed
3 tablespoons olive oil
3 garlic cloves, bashed
1 red onion, finely chopped
2 celery sticks, finely sliced
1 red (bell) pepper, cut into strips
1 yellow (bell) pepper, cut into strips
60 g/½ cup large green olives, bashed to help remove the stone/pit, then torn into chunks
40 g/4 tablespoons capers
50 g/⅓ cup pine nuts
25 g/2 tablespoons raisins
150 ml/⅔ cup tomato passata (or a good-quality jarred tomato sauce)
5 tablespoons red wine vinegar
1 tablespoon sugar
a bunch of fresh basil, roughly chopped

serves 2 as a starter/appetizer

For the marinated mozzarella, rip the mozzarella into rough chunks. Combine with the other ingredients and allow to marinate for 30 minutes.

Meanwhile, for the caponata, take a deep saucepan and pour in enough vegetable oil to come one third of the way up the pan. Heat the oil to 180°C (350°F). If by some miracle you have an oil thermometer, use this. If like me and every other normal person, you've never heard of one, just heat the oil until an aubergine/eggplant cube sizzles nicely without the oil bubbling too aggressively. Fry the aubergine/eggplant in batches until deep golden. Remove and allow to drain on kitchen paper/paper towel.

Heat the olive oil in a heavy-based pan or casserole dish. Add the garlic and fry until browned, then remove and set aside. Add the onion, celery, (bell) peppers, olives and capers. Fry until the onion is translucent and beginning to caramelize – about 10 minutes. Add the pine nuts and raisins and fry for 2 minutes. Add the tomato passata and stir to incorporate everything. Put the vinegar and sugar in a cup and stir to dissolve the sugar. Add to the pan and cook for 15 minutes, stirring. Season to taste, but don't wimp out, as it needs a bold amount of salt. Remove from the heat and allow to cool slightly before adding the basil.

Toast the bread, rub each slice twice with the halved garlic and layer some basil leaves over it (this helps stop the toast getting soggy). Spoon the caponata and marinated mozzarella over the top and serve.

There's something enticingly primeval about bone marrow: you start by delicately prising out the wobbly goodness with a fork and quickly descend into sucking straight from the bone. The salad is a bit of a hassle, as you have to pick the individual leaves off the stalks, but the results are well worth it, and the fragrant pepperiness of the herbs cuts through the marrow's richness.

Don't throw away the bones once you've finished – they can be used to make a lovely dark veal stock.

Roasted veal marrow with herb, caper & toasted almond salad

- 4–6 pieces centre-cut veal marrow bones, about 7.5 cm/3 inch long
- olive oil, for roasting and dressing
- 1 tablespoon whole almonds
- a small bunch of fresh flat leaf parsley, leaves only
- 4 sprigs fresh tarragon, leaves only
- leaves from a head of celery
- 1 teaspoon capers
- 1 shallot, very thinly sliced
- freshly squeezed juice of ½ lemon
- sea salt
- good-quality sourdough, to serve
- 1 garlic clove, halved

serves 2 as a starter/appetizer

Preheat the oven to 200°C (400°F) Gas 6. Brush the bones with a little olive oil and roast for 15–20 minutes. The marrow should be soft and glistening, but not melted.

Warm a non-stick frying pan/skillet over medium heat and add the almonds with a splash of olive oil. Toast them until they are golden brown, then remove from the pan and set aside to cool.

While they're cooking, mix your herb leaves together. If you have particularly large parsley or celery leaves you can give them a quick chop or two, but personally I like to keep them whole. Add the capers, almonds, sliced shallots (I said thinly sliced!) and stir.

Mix the lemon juice with some olive oil and sea salt to make the dressing.

Cut the sourdough into chunky slices and toast them. Once toasted, give them a couple of rubs with the garlic clove.

Once the bones are cooked, dress the herb leaves with the dressing and serve alongside the bones and toasted sourdough.

Tuna & melon tartare with paprika crisps

A stunningly simple recipe that works brilliantly as a light appetizer, especially on a hot summer's day when you feel like something clean and fresh. The crisps/chips are a great way to turn boring pitta bread into something a little more lively. They're pretty versatile and work well with all sorts of pre-dinner nibbles. Try them dipped in hoummus or topped with guacamole, smoked salmon and soured cream.

For the tuna tartare

- 150 g/5 oz. fresh tuna loin, sashimi grade
- ½ shallot, very finely chopped
- ½ medium-ripe avocado, finely diced
- 1 tomato, seeds and pulp removed, diced
- ½ tablespoon chopped fresh coriander/cilantro leaves
- ½ teaspoon chopped fresh mint leaves
- 25 g/1 oz. diced cantaloupe melon (about ½ wedge)
- ½ red chilli, finely chopped (optional)
- grated zest of ¼ lime
- olive oil, for drizzling
- sea salt and freshly ground black pepper
- rocket/arugula, to serve

For the paprika crisps/chips

- 2 white pitta breads
- ½ teaspoon smoked paprika, hot or mild
- 2 tablespoons olive oil (use a little more or less, according to taste)
- sea salt

serves 2 as a starter/appetizer

Preheat the oven to 220°C (425°F) Gas 7.

Start by making the paprika crisps/chips – you can make these a couple of hours in advance if you want, as they'll keep well. In a large bowl, mix the paprika with the olive oil and some salt. Cut the pitta bread into small triangles and toss them with the olive oil-paprika mixture until they are nicely coated. Put them on a baking sheet, making sure that you only have one layer, or they'll go soggy. Bake them in the oven until they have turned golden brown and lightly charred at the edges. It should take about 5 minutes, but keep a hawk eye on them – a moment's distraction and they'll turn to cinders. Once cooked, take them out and lay them out on a wire rack to cool and crisp up.

For the tartare, cut the tuna into small dice. I suggest 5-mm (¼-inch) cubes, but you can go smaller or larger if you like. Gently mix with all the remaining ingredients, taking care that the melon and avocado do not turn to mush. The aim is to have a well-combined mixture, with each of the components distinctly visible.

Serve the tartare simply spooned onto some rocket/arugula, or shaped with a ring mould if you want to show off, with a handful of paprika crisps/chips on the side.

Roast poussin stuffed with herbed cream cheese, sun-dried tomatoes & olives

I'm always surprised by how few poussin seem to find their way onto our plates. They're easy to cook, tend to be less dry than their larger counterparts, and are, in general, reasonably priced too. Plus there's the kiddie-like joy on everyone's face when they realize they're getting a whole mini chicken!

The stuffing is a great way of adding extra flavour to the bird and protecting the breast from any risk of drying out. It's a bit fiddly and requires a robust constitution (in other words, not for the squeamish).

2 oven-ready whole poussins
25 g/2 tablespoons softened butter

For the stuffing
150 g/5 oz. cream cheese
1 garlic clove, crushed
2 sun-dried tomatoes, chopped
20 g/¼ cup olives, pitted and chopped
1 teaspoon grated Parmesan
1 small bunch fresh basil, chopped
grated zest of ½ unwaxed lemon
10 ml/⅔ tablespoon olive oil
sea salt and freshly ground black pepper

a few toothpicks

serves 2

Preheat the oven to 200°C (400°F) Gas 6. Take the poussins out of the fridge so that they come to room temperature before cooking.

Prepare the stuffing by mixing together all the ingredients and seasoning with salt and pepper. If it is too stiff to work (it shouldn't be, but each brand can be a little different), loosen it with a dash of double/heavy cream.

Lay the birds down so that the cavity is facing you. Carefully use your fingers to prise away the breast skin from the flesh, creating a pocket for the stuffing.

Carefully push half the filling under the skin of each bird until it is evenly spread under the skin. Use some toothpicks to close the skin back up.

Rub the birds with the softened butter and season all over with salt and black pepper (this will help the skin to crisp up). Roast for 35 minutes, basting them with any juices halfway through. Remove and wrap each bird individually in kitchen foil and leave to rest, breast-side down, for a further 10 minutes before serving.

Chicken stuffed with asparagus, goats' cheese & sun-dried tomatoes

Chicken kiev for the landed gentry, this looks quite incredible when you slice it down the middle and reveal the cross-section of vibrant asparagus and sun-dried tomatoes. All the hard work can be done well in advance, leaving you free to sip a Riesling and lament the decline of the modern broadsheet newspaper.

For the chicken

4 asparagus stems
2 chicken breasts, skin removed and butterflied (cut in half lengthwise but not all the way through; if you're unsure, ask your butcher to help)
4 sun-dried tomatoes
4 slices Parma ham
100 g/3½ oz. goats' cheese
olive oil, for cooking

For the sauce

4 tablespoons pesto sauce
2 tablespoons crème fraîche
10 cherry tomatoes on the vine
fresh basil leaves, to decorate
rocket/arugula leaves, to serve

serves 2

Preheat the oven to 220°C (425°F) Gas 7.

Bring a pan of salted water to the boil, add the asparagus and cook for 3 minutes. Remove and refresh it under cold running water (or a bowl of iced water if you're a really dedicated pro). Once cooled, leave to dry.

Stuff each butterflied chicken breast with two asparagus stems placed lengthwise, two sun-dried tomatoes and half the goats' cheese, and season with salt and pepper. Close it up and wrap it in two slices of Parma ham. Secure with a toothpick if necessary.

Warm an ovenproof pan over high heat. For anyone who's wondering, ovenproof basically means that the handle is made of metal, not plastic.

Add a splash of olive oil to the pan and add the chicken breasts, skin-side down. Fry them until one side has crisped up a little. Flip them over and put the pan in the oven for a 15–20 minutes, or until the juices run clear. Put the cherry tomatoes in a small roasting pan and roast for 10–15 minutes, until the skins start to crack.

While it's cooking, mix together the pesto and crème fraîche, loosening it with a dash of hot water if it's too thick. It should be a thick but still pourable sauce.

Once the chicken is cooked, leave it to rest for 5 minutes before slicing horizontally, then arrange on a plate. Spoon the sauce over and serve with the cherry tomatoes, basil leaves and rocket/arugula.

Cod fillets with lemon & thyme crust & bean & chorizo stew

For the stew
3 tablespoons olive oil
120 g/4½ oz. cooking chorizo, cubed
2 red onions, finely chopped
2 garlic cloves, chopped
1 red (bell) pepper, finely chopped
1 fennel bulb, finely chopped
2 stalks celery, sliced
a sprig of fresh rosemary
1 x 400-g/14-oz. can butter/lima beans
200 ml/¾ cup vegetable stock/broth

For the fish
100 g/scant 1½ cups fresh breadcrumbs (see method)
leaves from 3–4 sprigs fresh thyme
grated zest of 1 unwaxed lemon
30 g/¼ cup pine nuts
2 skinless cod fillet pieces, approximately 200 g/7 oz. each, as thick as possible
flour, for dusting
2 eggs, lightly beaten
sea salt and freshly ground black pepper
2 lemon wedges, to serve

a food processor (optional)

serves 2

I'm not going to lie; this isn't a whip-it-up-while-the-ads-are-on kind of dish, but the results are well worth the effort and mess inherently involved in breadcrumbing anything. My advice? Prepare the beans a day or two in advance – they'll only get better, and it's one less thing to worry about on the night.

Preheat the oven to 200°C (400°F) Gas 6.

For the bean stew, heat the olive oil in a heavy-based saucepan over high heat. Fry the chorizo until crisp and its aromatic oil has been released. Remove and set aside for later.

Add the onions, garlic, pepper, fennel, celery and rosemary sprig. Fry over medium-high heat, stirring regularly, until the onions are beginning to brown – about 10 minutes.

Add the butter/lima beans and their juice (this helps to thicken up and flavour the stew). Add the stock/broth at the same time. Cook over high heat for 10 minutes, or until some of the liquid has reduced. Remove from the heat and add the fried chorizo.

For the fish, if you haven't got a food processor, use ready-made dried breadcrumbs. If you have got one, get some crusty white bread and break it up into small chunks. Pulse in the processor until you have large crumbs about the size of a large snowflake.

Mix the fresh or dried breadcrumbs with the thyme leaves, lemon zest, pine nuts and season with salt and pepper.

Get three bowls ready. Add some flour to one, the eggs to another, and the breadcrumbs to the last one.

The idea with the breadcrumbs is to substitute a breadcrumb crust for the cod's real skin, so you only want to breadcrumb one side of the fillet. Press one side into the flour, then the eggs, and finally the breadcrumbs. Push it down firmly so that as many breadcrumbs as possible stick to the cod. If it looks like you haven't got a good crust, just dip it back into the egg mixture and the breadcrumbs once more.

Warm a non-stick, ovenproof pan over medium-high heat. Heat a good splash of olive oil and fry the cod, crust-side down, for a couple of minutes, or until it has just started to brown. Turn the cod over and put the pan in the oven. Cook for a further 10–15 minutes. If the crust looks like it's getting too brown, just cover it loosely with some foil.

Serve the cod with the warm bean stew and a wedge of lemon.

I should feel sorry for mussels. Everyone's so busy fretting about how to cook a live lobster humanely that they've forgotten all about the countless mussels being steamed alive every day. After spending most of my first month as a chef scraping barnacles off mussels' backs, however, I have developed a deep-rooted and frankly sinister antipathy towards them. It's probably why I love to cook them so much.

Mussel, cannellini & pancetta soup with rosemary oil

For the rosemary oil
2 tablespoons olive oil
1 sprig fresh rosemary

For the mussels
1⅓ tablespoons olive oil
1 white onion, chopped
500 g/1 lb. 2 oz. mussels, scraped and de-bearded
50 ml/scant ¼ cup white wine

For the soup base
2 tablespoons olive oil
60 g/2¼ oz. cubed pancetta
30 g/2 tablespoons butter
2 garlic cloves, chopped
2 stalks celery, chopped
2 white onions, chopped
2 small carrots, chopped
1 small bunch fresh flat leaf parsley, leaves and stalks chopped
2 sprigs fresh rosemary, stalks removed
2 x 400-g/14-oz. cans cannellini beans in water

a hand-held electric blender or jug blender

serves 2

Prepare the rosemary oil by putting the olive oil and the rosemary (stalks included) in a frying pan/skillet. Warm over medium heat until the rosemary has darkened. Set aside to cool.

For the mussels, heat the olive oil in a deep pan set over a high heat and add the onion. Fry for about 5 minutes, until lightly caramelized, then add the mussels and white wine. Cover with a lid and steam over high heat until the shells have opened. Set a colander over a bowl and drain the mussels, being sure to keep the liquid for later. Discard any mussels that remain closed. Keep a few to one side for decorating the dish, remove the rest from their shells and set aside.

For the soup base, warm a heavy-based pan over medium heat and add the oil and pancetta. Fry the pancetta until the fat has rendered and the cubes are nicely crispy, then remove them with a slotted spoon and set aside. Add the butter, garlic, celery, onions, carrots, parsley and rosemary. Gently fry for 10 minutes, until beginning to brown. Add the cannellini beans along with their water and the reserved juice from cooking the mussels. Cover and cook over low heat for 20 minutes, or until the beans are beginning to disintegrate. Liquidize the soup with a hand-held electric blender or jug blender until it is a smooth, unctuous consistency. Add the fried pancetta, shelled mussels and a few turns of the pepper mill and season with salt to taste.

Serve with a generous drizzle of rosemary oil and a few mussels in their shells to decorate.

Pot-cooked beef fillet with pea purée & hasselback potatoes

For the beef
1 piece beef fillet, about 350–400 g/12–14 oz.
1 garlic clove, crushed
olive oil, for cooking and marinating
1½ tablespoons sake
1½ tablespoons ketjap manis (available from most Asian markets)
1½ tablespoons tamari soy
50 g/3½ tablespoons cold butter, cubed
butter, for cooking

For the hasselback potatoes
2 large roasting potatoes
1½ tablespoons olive oil
1 garlic clove, crushed
½ teaspoon chopped fresh thyme
sea salt and freshly ground black pepper

For the pea purée
15 g/1 tablespoon butter
½ white onion, chopped
200 g/7 oz. frozen peas (the small petit pois type)
45 ml/3 tablespoons vegetable stock/broth
a small bunch of fresh mint
1 tablespoon double/heavy cream

a large, deep cast-iron casserole dish, big enough to fit the whole fillet
a hand-held electric blender

serves 2

I'm generally sceptical when it comes to fillet of beef. It's one of the least flavourful cuts (as a rough rule of thumb, the more work a muscle does, the tougher it is to eat but the more flavour it has. Game is a good example). In the wrong hands, fillet can be a drab, dry affair, made even more depressing by the sound of the butcher laughing all the way to the bank. So fillet was strictly off the menu until I was introduced to this recipe by Belinda (that's Mrs K. to you), the mother of a lifelong friend, and one of the most effortlessly talented cooks I know.

Preheat the oven to 200°C (400°F) Gas 6.

Prepare the beef fillet by rubbing it with the crushed garlic and a little olive oil. Pour over the sake, ketjap manis and tamari soy. Marinate in the fridge for a couple of hours or overnight. Take it out of the fridge at least an hour before cooking so it can come to room temperature.

Scrub the potatoes, but do not peel them. With a sharp knife, make horizontal cuts at 5-mm (¼-inch) intervals all the way along, without slicing all the way through.

Mix the olive oil, crushed garlic, thyme and salt and pepper. Spoon a little of this over each potato. Arrange them in a roasting pan and spoon over any remaining olive oil. Season the potatoes generously and bake for 45 minutes–1 hour, until all the slices have fanned out and the potato is crisp and golden brown.

For the peas, melt the butter in a pan and cook the onion gently for 15 minutes. Add the frozen peas and vegetable stock/broth, bring to the boil and cook for a further 5 minutes. Add the fresh mint and cream, then blitz with a hand-held electric blender or food processor.

Now for the beef. Heat a little butter and olive oil in a heavy-based casserole dish over medium-high heat. Remove the beef from the marinade (reserving the marinade) and brown it on all sides in the pan. Once browned, reduce the heat to medium and cover with a lid, leaving a small gap for steam to escape. Cook for about 20 minutes, then remove the beef from the pan and cover with kitchen foil. Pour the marinade into the casserole and warm it. When hot, add the cubes of cold butter and whisk briskly to thicken the sauce. Once all the butter is incorporated, remove the pan from the heat. Once cooled a little, return the beef and allow it to sit in the sauce, absorbing the flavour, for a further 20 minutes. To serve, remove the meat and slice it thinly. Warm the sauce gently and spoon it over the sliced meat. Serve with the potatoes, pea purée and extra sauce.

Ossobuco with orange gremolata

I really don't understand why this cut of meat doesn't crop up in more restaurants. It's cheap, hearty, easy to cook, and every time we put it on the menu it flies out of the kitchen. Personally, I think it's a PR problem: it's pretty much exclusively known by its Italian name, *ossobuco*, which scares chefs into thinking that it's only suitable for an Italian restaurant. Balls to that. Admittedly, 'cross-cut veal shank' doesn't trip off the tongue, but it's a great cut of meat that's suitable for all sorts of slow-cooked dishes. Try making a curry with it – the bone helps thicken up the sauce and the meat is meltingly tender.

This is a relatively traditional recipe and a good introduction to the meat, but don't stop at this – experiment with it.

For the ossobuco
flour, for dusting
2 x ossobuco (cross-cut veal shanks), about 300 g/11 oz. each
vegetable oil, for frying
100 ml/⅓ cup olive oil
1 small white onion, chopped
1 garlic clove, chopped
1 small carrot, chopped
1 stalk celery, thinly sliced
½ small bulb fennel, chopped
100 ml/⅓ cup red wine
1 sprig fresh rosemary
1 bay leaf
400 g/14 oz. canned chopped tomatoes (or Tomato & Basil sauce, see page 132)
about 250 ml/1 cup beef stock/broth
sea salt and freshly ground black pepper
mashed Désirée potatoes or polenta, to serve

For the orange gremolata
grated zest of ½ unwaxed orange and ½ unwaxed lemon
a small bunch of flat leaf parsley, roughly chopped
½ garlic clove, finely chopped

serves 2

Season the flour with a little salt and pepper, then toss your ossobuco in it, making sure they are nicely coated.

Heat a heavy-based pan or casserole dish over high heat. Add a splash of vegetable oil and fry the ossobuco for about 3 minutes each side, until nicely browned all over. Don't overcrowd the pan; you want to caramelize the outside of the meat, not steam it.

Remove the ossobuco and set aside. Empty out the pan and give it a quick wash if there are any burnt bits stuck to it. Heat it up again over medium heat and add the olive oil, onion, garlic, carrot, celery and fennel. Cook for about 10 minutes, or until the onions are beginning to brown.

Add the red wine, rosemary and bay leaf. Bring to the boil and allow to simmer away until reduced by half. Add the tomatoes, ossobuco and half the beef stock/broth. Bring to a simmer, then reduce the heat to its lowest setting and simmer for 1½–2 hours. Add a little more beef stock/broth if the sauce seems to be thickening too much as it cooks. You want the meat to be meltingly soft, but still just attached to the bone.

Prepare the orange gremolata by mixing together all the ingredients and loosening it with a little olive oil.

Serve the ossobuco on a bed of creamy mashed Désirée potatoes or polenta, with the gremolata spooned on top.

This is a simple, everyday pasta that's not particularly cheffy, nor is it the height of edible aesthetics. It's just damn good comfort food, perfect for eating in on a night in curled up on the sofa watching trashy TV. Make more than you think; you'll undoubtedly have a second portion, and quite possibly a third straight from the fridge during the ad break.

Spaghetti all'amatriciana

250 g/9 oz. good-quality spaghetti
vegetable oil, for frying
50 g/2 oz. cubed pancetta
50 ml/scant ¼ cup olive oil
1 garlic clove, bashed but left whole
1 white onion, finely chopped
250 ml/1 cup Tomato & Basil sauce (see page 132)
30 g/1¼ oz. grated Parmesan, plus extra to serve
a small bunch of fresh basil, roughly chopped
mascarpone, to serve

serves 2

Bring a large pan of water to the boil and add salt. Add the pasta and cook according to the instructions on the packet, subtracting 1 minute.

While the pasta is cooking, heat a large non-stick frying pan/skillet over medium-high heat with a splash of vegetable oil. Fry the pancetta cubes until nicely crispy, then remove. Discard the cooking oil and carefully give the pan a quick wipe with a kitchen towel/paper towel (don't burn yourself!).

Return the pan to the heat and add the olive oil and garlic. Fry the garlic until browned all over, then remove from the pan with a slotted spoon. You want it to flavour the oil, but not stay so long that it becomes bitter. Add the onions and fry until translucent and lightly caramelized, then add the Tomato & Basil Sauce. Warm the sauce through, then remove from the heat. Add the Parmesan, pancetta and basil leaves.

When the pasta is almost cooked but still very much al dente, tip it into a colander, reserving one mugful of the cooking water for use later. Return the pasta to the pan and add the sauce. Return to low heat and stir, adding a little of the cooking water if it's too thick. Effectively, you're finishing cooking the pasta in the sauce, which means it will absorb much more of the flavour.

Serve with a sprinkling of extra Parmesan, a few basil leaves, and a spoon of mascarpone on top.

Butterflied prawns with avocado, harissa & yogurt

A very simple, light dish that packs a hefty punch. You can make your own harissa paste but it is just as delicious straight from the jar. I strongly advise wearing food-safe vinyl gloves when preparing the chillies if you do make your own; no matter how diligently you wash your hands, there will always be some lingering spice on your fingers, which will cause agony if you rub your eyes. Suffice it to say that I learned this the hard way…

4 large raw tiger prawns/ jumbo shrimp, about 100 g/3½ oz. each
1 small avocado, sliced
½ small red onion, sliced
a small bunch of fresh mint
1 head little gem lettuce
olive oil, to serve
sea salt, to taste
½ lemon, cut into wedges

For the dressing
1–2 teaspoons harissa paste
2 tablespoons yogurt

serves 2

Preheat a heavy-based grill pan over high heat.

Put the tiger prawns/jumbo shrimp on a chopping/cutting board and cut them lengthwise with a sharp serrated knife from the tail to just before the head. Open up the tail and season with a little olive oil and salt.

Once the pan is smoking hot, add the prawns/shrimp so that they stand on their opened-up tails. Cook for 3–5 minutes, until the flesh has turned white, then turn off the heat.

Mix the avocado, red onion, mint and lettuce and drizzle with a little olive oil and sea salt. Place the prawns/shrimp on top with a wedge of lemon.

Depending on how fiery you like it, mix 2 teaspoons of harissa paste with the yogurt (the yogurt counteracts the chilli heat) and dress the prawns and avocado salad. Or you could put a dollop of yogurt and a spoonful of harissa on each plate and let your guest manage their own heat.

on the side

Side dishes are the unsung heroes of the culinary world. Everyone loves to wax lyrical about their main course/entrée, but the humble accompaniments barely get a look-in. There's a standing ovation for the 'meltingly succulent organic Barbary duck breast, glistening in a juniper jus', while the humble side of mashed potatoes, a labour of love in itself, is given a patronizing 'oh yes, very nice, not dry at all'. We might as well give it a pat on the head and a lollipop for being such a good boy.

Just because they're not the star of the show doesn't mean that sides aren't important. A meal simply wouldn't function without sides. A good parallel can be found in any professional kitchen in the form of the tireless and forever under-appreciated kitchen porter. For those of you unfamiliar with kitchen porters, they're the ones who spend hour after hour huddled over the sink scrubbing pans and washing plates, and once the rush of a service is finished and the chefs are enjoying a well-earned beer, the kitchen porter has to slave away with broom and mop until the kitchen is gleaming. It's a thankless task, made all the harder by the shameful treatment they often receive at the hands of chefs who are drunk on the petty hierarchy of a restaurant kitchen (something we have never tolerated at Megan's). It might sound like a fairly easy job, with no real training needed, surely nowhere near as important as the chefs who actually make the food? Well, it's certainly not easy, and believe me, if you lose your kitchen porter in the middle of service you're in a world of pain.

Sides, like kitchen porters, are an integral part of the whole, and they deserve as much respect as any other part. You can have the best roast chump of lamb in the world but it would bland and dreary be without any sides to add variety and different textures. While you might choose a new main dish every night, it's the sides you'll be going back to time and time again, so please raise a glass to sides and kitchen porters alike, for without them our dinners just wouldn't be the same.

Creamed spinach

There's a classic way to make creamed spinach that involves a *roux* – and then there's the easy way. This takes just a few minutes, and tastes amazing. We use a dash of English mustard to add a little sharpness, but feel free to use Dijon or wholegrain, or just leave it out.

olive oil, for frying
2 garlic cloves, chopped
500 g/1 lb. 2 oz. fresh spinach, washed
200 ml/¾ cup double/heavy cream
1 teaspoon English mustard
sea salt and freshly ground black pepper

serves 4

Heat a large pan that's big enough to hold all the spinach over high heat. Add a good splash of olive oil and fry the garlic. When it's just beginning to colour, add all the spinach along with a pinch of salt. Cook, stirring, until it has wilted down. Cook for a minute or so, until some of the excess water has bubbled off. Add the cream and mustard and cook for a further 3–5 minutes, or until you have reached your desired consistency. Check the seasoning and serve.

Perfect mash

There are countless recipes for mash out there, and no doubt each of their creators think that their mash is perfect, just like me. The truth of the matter is that everyone likes a different type of mash. Some prefer a drier, clumpier mash; others prefer a looser, more malleable one. My mother likes to make hers in a blender, for some reason (I strongly advise you not to go down that route). For me, mash should be sensuously rich and velvety smooth.

1 kg/2¼ lbs. Désirée potatoes
200 ml/¾ cup double/heavy cream
125 g/1 stick plus 1 tablespoon butter
sea salt and freshly ground black pepper

serves 4–6

Cut the potatoes into equal chunks. Unless they are monster ones or particularly runty, I would simply quarter them. Put them in a pan and cover with cold water. Add a good dash of salt (about the same amount you would use when cooking pasta) and bring to the boil. Cook until a knife passes through them with little or no resistance.

In the meantime, put the cream and butter in a pan and heat until the butter has melted. Add a good few turns of the pepper mill and a hefty pinch of salt.

Once the potatoes are cooked, drain them in a colander and allow them to steam for a minute or so, but no more. Mash the potatoes any way you can – you get the smoothest results by pushing them through a fine sieve, but you have to be a Michelin-starred chef or heavily obsessive to go to those lengths. A vegetable mouli or potato ricer will give fantastic results, or a standard potato masher will be fine, although you'll never get all the lumps out, no matter how hard you try.

Combine the melted cream and butter with the potatoes and stir until it is all incorporated. Check the seasoning and serve.

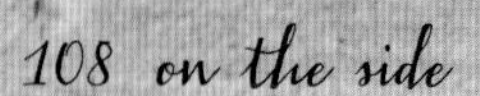

Roasted cauliflower with walnuts, dates & parsley

I was introduced to this recipe by a long-time American friend when we were all staying with a friend in the Swiss mountains for New Year. There were only three food shops, each with an eye-watering selection of cheese but precious little else. She was insistent that she wanted to cook this recipe. Now I challenge you to find dates in a remote Swiss mountain village – it's no mean feat! I suggested a million alternatives (raisins, dried cranberries), but she was absolutely adamant that it had to be dates, and how right she was.

1 large cauliflower, broken into florets
olive oil, for roasting
75 g/5 tablespoons butter
50 g/½ cup walnuts, roughly chopped
1 garlic clove, crushed
50 g/½ cup pitted dates, roughly chopped
1 small bunch fresh flat leaf parsley, chopped
sea salt and freshly ground black pepper

serves 4–6

Preheat the oven to 200°C (400°F) Gas 6.

Toss the cauliflower florets in a little olive oil and season with salt and pepper. Roast in the oven for 20–30 minutes, or until they are golden brown with lightly charred edges.

Melt the butter in a pan over medium heat. Add the walnuts and toast for 5 minutes, then add the crushed garlic and dates. Reduce the heat to low and continue to cook for 5 minutes.

Mix the roasted cauliflower with the date-nut mixture, scatter with chopped parsley and serve.

Sherried parsnips with chestnuts & bacon

A virtually foolproof recipe that always amazes. Cooking the parsnips in sherry renders them meltingly soft with a rich, savoury-sweet glaze. The chestnuts and bacon add a little bit of bite.

olive oil, for frying
100 g/3½ oz. cubed bacon lardons
100 g/¾ cup peeled cooked chestnuts, roughly chopped
600 g/1 lb. 5 oz. parsnips, cut into thick batons
75 g/5 tablespoons butter
200 ml/¾ cup cream sherry
½ small bunch fresh flat-leaf parsley

serves 4

Warm a frying pan/skillet over medium-high heat. Add a good splash of olive oil and the bacon. Fry until the bacon is crisp and the fat has rendered. Remove the bacon with a slotted spoon and add the chestnuts. Fry until golden brown, then remove and set aside.

Put the parsnips and butter in another pan. Pour over the sherry until they are just covered. Put the pan over high heat and bring to the boil, then reduce the heat to a low simmer and cook, uncovered, until a knife will pass through the parsnips easily. Remove the parsnips and increase the heat to boil the sherry until it has reduced to a loose syrup. Return the parsnips to the pan and shake until they are nicely glazed. Serve with the chestnuts, bacon and parsley sprinkled on top.

Roasted butternut squash

There's something so homely and comforting about butternut – it has all the unctuousness of a good mash without ever feeling heavy or cloying in the mouth.

olive oil, for toasting
40 g/⅓ cup shelled skinned pistachio nuts
1 large butternut squash, halved, seeds removed, cut into large crescents
3 sprigs fresh rosemary, roughly chopped
1 large red chilli, chopped
sea salt and freshly ground black pepper

serves 4

Preheat the oven to 200°C (400°F) Gas 6.

Heat a pan over high heat with a little olive oil and toast the pistachios, stirring, until they turn a greeny golden brown. In a large bowl, combine the butternut and rosemary with a good splash of olive oil, salt and pepper. Place a roasting pan large enough to hold the squash in a single layer in the oven for 5 minutes to heat. This will help the butternut caramelize when cooking.

Add the butternut to the pan and roast for 25 minutes. Give the pan a few good shakes halfway through cooking. Remove and sprinkle the chopped chilli over the butternut, then return to the oven to bake for 5 more minutes. Scatter the pistachios on the top and serve.

Cannellini beans with rosemary & bay

A rich, warming side that's ideal for a cold winter's night. It's pretty versatile; it's great with roast lamb, or extend it with good stock/broth for a rich soup.

50 ml/scant ¼ cup olive oil
2 garlic cloves, bashed
2 red onions, finely chopped
2 celery stalks, sliced
1 carrot, finely chopped
1 small bunch fresh flat leaf parsley, stalks and leaves chopped
2 x 400-g/14-oz. cans cannellini beans in water
150 ml/⅔ cup vegetable stock/broth
50 ml/scant ¼ cup white wine
3 sprigs fresh rosemary
4 bay leaves
50g/¼ cup finely grated Parmesan cheese
sea salt and freshly ground black pepper

serves 8–10

Heat the oil in a pan over medium heat. Add the garlic and fry until browned on both sides. Remove and set aside.

Add the onions, celery, carrot, parsley stalks and leaves. Throw in a good pinch of salt and fry until the onion is turning translucent and beginning to brown at the edges.

Add the cannellini beans along with their water, the stock, white wine, rosemary and bay. Bring to the boil and simmer for 20 minutes. Remove from the heat, allow to cool for 5 minutes, then add the grated Parmesan and check the seasoning. Beans will always taste best at ambient temperature, or as close as possible, so try and leave them to cool for a short while before serving.

Jerusalem artichoke & mushroom purée

I have a soft spot for Jerusalem artichokes. They have a charming mangy-dog look to them, all gnarled and begging to be loved. As you will no doubt have read in other cookbooks, they have no link whatsoever to Jerusalem, but they do have the most wonderful artichokey flavour.

500 g/1 lb. 2 oz. Jerusalem artichokes, peeled and halved
100 g/3½ oz./7 tablespoons butter
1 red onion, chopped
1 teaspoon chopped fresh thyme
250 g/9 oz. wild mushrooms, chopped
2 garlic cloves, sliced
200 ml/scant ¾ cup white wine
75 ml/scant ⅓ cup double/heavy cream
freshly squeezed juice of ½ lemon
sea salt and freshly ground black pepper

a hand-held electric blender or food processor

serves 4–6

Put the Jerusalem artichokes in a pan of cold water. Bring to the boil and cook for around 30 minutes, or until they are tender and a knife passes through them easily. Drain and set aside.

Set a pan over medium-low heat and melt the butter. Add the chopped onion, thyme and a good few twists of the salt and pepper mill. Cook for about 8–10 minutes, stirring frequently, until the onions have started to caramelize.

Add the Jerusalem artichokes, wild mushrooms and garlic. Increase the heat and fry until the artichokes and mushrooms are beginning to turn golden.

Add the wine and allow it to reduce by half, then add the cream and lemon juice. Bring to the boil and blitz with a hand-held blender. Check the seasoning and serve. It goes very well with roasted chicken.

Minted pea purée

Basically 'mushy peas' with good publicity. Vibrant green and deceptively unctuous, it pairs especially well with lamb and fish.

50 g/3½ tablespoons butter
1 white onion, chopped
600 g/4¾ cups frozen peas (the petit pois type)
125 ml/½ cup vegetable stock/broth
a small bunch of fresh mint
50 ml/scant ¼ cup double/heavy cream
sea salt and freshly ground black pepper

a hand-held electric blender or food processor

serves 4

Melt the butter in a pan and cook the onion gently for 15 minutes or so. Add the frozen peas and vegetable stock/broth. Bring to the boil and cook for 5 more minutes. Add the fresh mint and cream, season with salt and pepper, then blitz with a hand blender or in a food processor and serve.

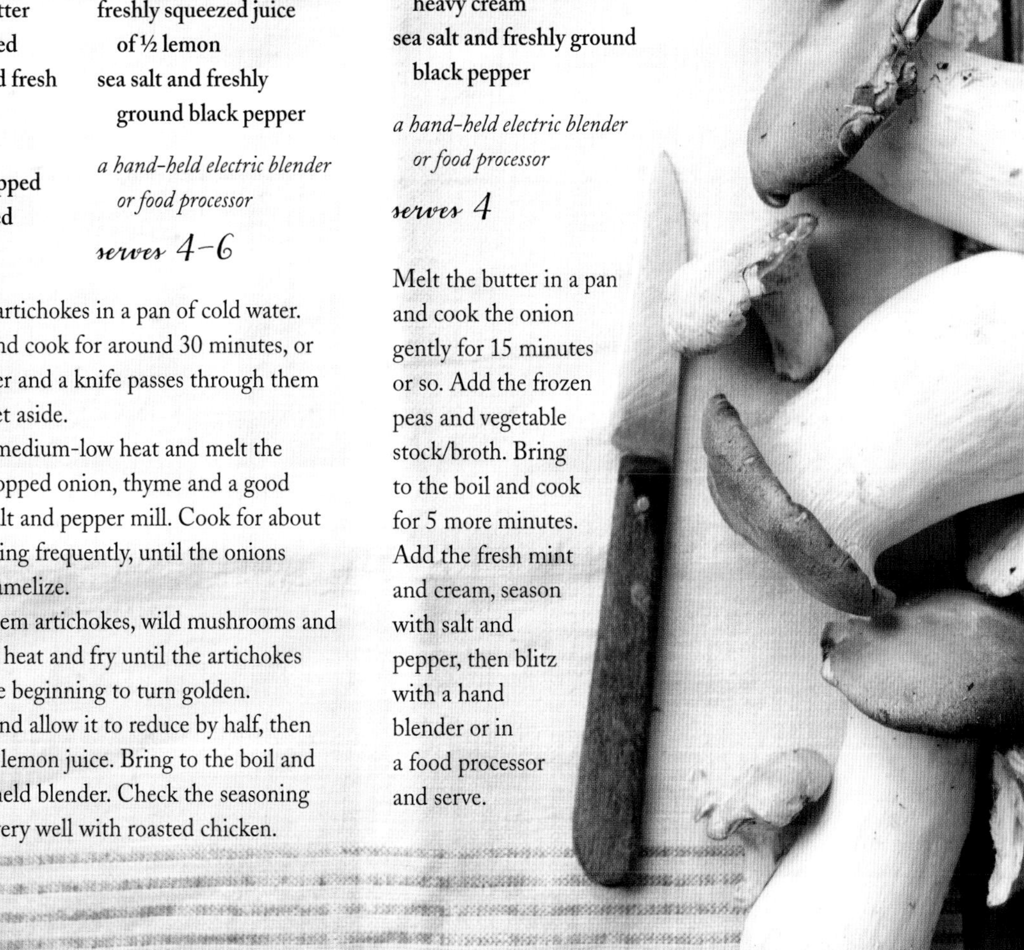

Grilled courgettes with basil, mint & lemon

An elegant side that's perfect for a light lunch or paired with grilled meat. I advise using a mandolin slicer; it's a worthy investment. It will give you a nasty cut at least once in your life, guaranteed, but you'll heal.

4 courgettes/zucchini, sliced lengthwise
olive oil, for brushing
1 garlic clove, crushed
grated zest and freshly squeezed juice of 1 unwaxed lemon
2–3 sprigs fresh mint leaves, chopped
a small bunch of fresh basil, chopped
sea salt and freshly ground black pepper
a handful of roasted hazelnuts

a ridged grill pan or barbecue

serves 4

Warm a ridged grill pan or barbecue until it's smoking hot. Brush the courgette/zucchini slices with olive oil and cook on both sides until nicely charred. Remove from the pan.

Mix together the crushed garlic, lemon juice, mint, half the basil and a good glug of olive oil. Pour over the grilled courgettes/zucchini. Scatter with the remaining basil, roasted hazelnuts and the lemon zest. Season with salt and pepper and serve.

Cheesy French beans

Creamy blue cheese and crunchy green beans is a great pairing that works equally well as a hot side or as a cold salad.

50 g/½ cup walnut halves
olive oil, for frying
200 ml/¾ cup double/heavy cream
100 g/3½ oz. Gorgonzola
200 g/7 oz. French beans

serves 4

Bring a pan of salted water to the boil.

Heat a pan over medium heat. Add the walnuts with a splash of olive oil and toast them until golden brown. Remove and set aside to cool.

Put the cream and Gorgonzola in another pan and warm over low heat until the Gorgonzola had melted. Don't allow it to boil or you'll destroy the consistency. Add the walnuts and remove from the heat.

Cook the green beans in the boiling water for 3–5 minutes, until just tender but still crunchy. There's nothing worse than a limp school-dinner bean.

Pour the sauce on top and serve.

Béarnaise sauce

We always serve béarnaise sauce with our *côte de boeuf*, and it's simply unbeatable with steak. It can prove a little challenging, as it will split if it gets too hot or you add the butter too fast. Keep trying, as it's well worth the curses and foot stamping.

Ideally, use tarragon vinegar instead of white wine vinegar. It's absurdly easy to make: get a couple of bunches of fresh tarragon, cover with white wine vinegar, seal in an airtight jar and leave somewhere cool and dark for a couple of weeks.

2 tablespoons white wine vinegar
1 shallot, diced
2 egg yolks
250 g/2 sticks plus 1 tablespoon butter, melted
¼ teaspoon cayenne pepper
2 tablespoons chopped fresh tarragon
sea salt

serves 4

Put the vinegar and shallot in a non-reactive pan and bring to the boil. Simmer until the vinegar has reduced by a third, then pour the contents into a large heatproof bowl.

Set the bowl over a pan of boiling water. Make sure the water isn't touching the base of the bowl, or you risk scrambling the eggs. Add the egg yolks and whisk to combine with the vinegar. While whisking continuously, pour in the melted butter in a slow stream. Once all the butter has been emulsified, add the cayenne pepper and chopped tarragon. If it is very thick (it should be pourable, but only just), add a splash of hot water.

The sauce should remain emulsified as long as you keep it at an ambient or slightly higher temperature. Should the mixture split at any point, you can try and save it by warming a couple of tablespoons of double/heavy cream to just below boiling point, then slowly pouring in the split mixture, whisking frantically.

Garlic & parsley butter

A classic recipe, which is prone to many different interpretations. There's something quintessentially 1970s about it, some undeniable kitsch. I love it.

You'll be very grateful for a stand mixer here.

250 g/2 sticks plus 1 tablespoon salted butter, softened
3 garlic cloves, crushed
1 large bunch fresh flat leaf parsley, chopped

a stand mixer (optional)

serves 8

Spoon the butter into a large bowl or a stand mixer. Using a wooden spoon or the paddle attachment, beat the butter until it is several shades lighter and has grown noticeably in volume. Stir in the garlic and parsley and chill in the fridge until set.

Salsa rossa

A punchy, summery salsa that's great for just about any Mediterranean-style grilled dish.

6 tomatoes, pulp and seeds removed, chopped
1 red (bell) pepper, chopped
1 yellow (bell) pepper, chopped
1 red onion, chopped
a bunch of fresh basil, chopped
1 garlic clove, finely chopped
1 red chilli, chopped (optional)
olive oil, to taste
sea salt and freshly ground black pepper

serves 8

Mix together all the ingredients, season to taste and top with olive oil until you reach your desired consistency.

Tomato & coriander salsa

A zingy salsa with a good old kick, this is great with grilled fish or tortilla chips as an alternative to depressing, mass-produced Mexican salsa.

6 tomatoes, chopped
a small bunch of fresh coriander/cilantro, roughly chopped
½ garlic clove, very finely chopped or crushed
2 tablespoons white wine vinegar
150 ml/⅔ cup olive oil
½ teaspoon Tabasco sauce
sea salt and freshly ground black pepper

serves 8

Mix all the ingredients together and season to taste.

Salsa verde

An amazingly versatile sauce that pairs well with almost anything, although it's particularly well suited to white fish and lamb.

a large bunch of fresh flat leaf parsley
a small bunch of fresh basil
2 sprigs fresh tarragon
the leaves from a head of celery
1 tablespoon capers, roughly chopped
1 small red onion, finely chopped
3 anchovy fillets, roughly chopped
1 garlic clove, crushed
1 red chilli, chopped (optional)
1 teaspoon Dijon mustard
2 tablespoons red wine vinegar
olive oil, to taste
sea salt and freshly ground black pepper

serves 8

Chop all the leaves, then add the rest of the ingredients except the olive oil. It's up to you how coarse or fine you want the sauce, but personally I prefer it rough so you can see all the different ingredients. Mix well.

Pour in olive oil to your liking. Generally speaking, the oil should cover the chopped ingredients, but only just. Stir again and season to taste.

Reduced balsamic vinaigrette

Balsamic vinegar had all the hallmarks of a fad, and I was sure it was going to quickly move from cliché to passé. But it looks like it's here to stay, and quite right too; it's a unique flavour. There are many different types, with varying taste, viscosity, and, of course, price. The most expensive ones are usually thick and syrupy with a concentrated flavour, which you can replicate simply by reducing your standard balsamic in a hot pan.

125 ml/½ cup ordinary balsamic vinegar
125 ml/½ cup olive oil
1 teaspoon clear honey
1 teaspoon Dijon mustard
freshly squeezed juice of ½ lemon
sea salt

serves 8

Put the balsamic in a pan and bring to the boil. Reduce by half, then test for viscosity by pouring a drop onto a cold plate. It should be syrupy but still pourable, the same consistency as maple syrup. If you reduce it too far it will become a solid blob upon cooling.

Put the reduced balsamic into a jar with the remaining ingredients and a good pinch of salt. Close the jar tightly and shake.

Red chilli, garlic & thyme vinaigrette

A powerful sauce that's especially good with seafood. Try adding it to a pan of frying tiger prawns/shrimp just before the end of cooking.

100 ml/⅓ cup olive oil
2 garlic cloves
2 large red chillis
125 g/1 stick plus 1 tablespoon butter
2 fresh thyme sprigs, chopped
200 ml/¾ cup white wine
sea salt and freshly ground black pepper

a food processor

serves 8

Combine the olive oil, garlic and chilli in a food processor and blend to a paste.

Melt the butter in a frying pan/skillet over medium-high heat. Add the chilli-garlic paste and thyme. Fry for 5 minutes, stirring regularly so it doesn't catch and burn.

Add the white wine, bring to the boil and reduce by half. Season boldly with salt and pepper.

Guacamole

Everyone loves guacamole, and rightly so, but it deserves more than just Dorito chips and fajitas. Try combining it with smoked salmon and sour cream on toasted sourdough. Damn, it's good!

I like the ingredients to stand up and be counted, so I chop them coarsely, but you can go finer if you prefer.

3 avocados, ripe but not blackened or bruised
1 tomato, deseeded and chopped
1 red onion, chopped
1 garlic clove, crushed
a bunch of fresh coriander/cilantro, chopped
1 large red chilli, chopped
freshly squeezed juice of ½ lime
30 ml/2 tablespoons olive oil
sea salt

serves 8

Chop one of the avocados into rough pieces and set aside. Mash the other two until you have a coarse paste. Combine all the ingredients and season boldly.

If you feel like a bit of a change, try toasting some grated coconut and sprinkling on top.

Pedro's onion & paprika salsa

An exceptionally simple salsa that's perfect for grilled meat or white fish. It's best to make it a day or so in advance so that the flavours have time to mingle.

1 white onion, finely chopped
2 garlic cloves, crushed
2 teaspoons hot paprika
75 ml/scant ⅓ cup olive oil
2 tablespoons white wine vinegar
1 tablespoon chopped fresh flat leaf parsley
sea salt and freshly ground black pepper

serves 8

Mix all the ingredients except the parsley, season with salt and pepper and leave to sit for a few hours. Stir in the chopped parsley a couple of hours before serving.

Saffron aioli

Making aioli was how I learned the importance of seasoning. It will taste of virtually nothing if not seasoned properly, so don't be shy. Traditional aioli is made with raw garlic, but I find it can become overpowering. If you like it garlicky, just add one or two cloves of crushed raw garlic instead of the roasted. It's great with fish and seafood, but I like to spread it on toasted sourdough and top with fried chorizo. Healthy, no. Delicious, yes.

150 ml/⅔ cup olive oil
1 whole head garlic
1 small pinch (about ¼ teaspoon) saffron threads
1 tablespoon hot water
30 g/⅓ cup flaked/sliced almonds
2 egg yolks
1 teaspoon Dijon mustard
150 ml/⅔ cup vegetable oil
freshly squeezed juice of ½ lemon
sea salt and freshly ground black pepper

a food processor (optional)

fills a 455 g/ 1 lb jar

Preheat the oven to 220°C (425°F) Gas 7. Drizzle a little olive oil on the garlic bulb and wrap it in kitchen foil. Roast for 30 minutes, then remove and leave to cool. Add the saffron to the hot water and steep for 10 minutes.

Heat a pan over medium heat with a splash of oil. Add the almonds and toast until golden brown. Leave them whole or pulse them to a course powder, as you prefer.

In the food processor bowl or large mixing bowl, combine the egg yolk, mustard, saffron and half the water it has been steeped in. Start blending/whisking, pouring in the vegetable oil in a slow and steady stream, mixing all the time. Don't add it too fast or you'll end up with a curdled mixture. It should emulsify with the egg yolk to make a thick paste. Next, slowly add the olive oil. If it looks too thick, add a splash of saffron water. Once all the oil has been added, add the roasted garlic (give the foil a few pricks and squeeze; it should come out easily). Add the lemon juice and toasted almonds, then season boldly.

Hazelnut picada

A delicious, crunchy mixture that can be sprinkled on virtually anything. It goes particularly well with grilled/broiled pork. Be sure to add it at the last minute or it will soak up any liquids in the vicinity and go soggy.

Once prepared it should last for a good week or so. Store it in an airtight container out of the fridge, otherwise it will quickly lose its bite.

100 ml/⅓ cup olive oil
2 slices rustic white bread (ideally sourdough)
4 garlic cloves, bashed
100 g/¾ cup shelled skinned hazelnuts
1 sprig fresh rosemary, chopped
1 red chilli (optional), finely chopped
grated zest of ½ unwaxed orange
1 sprig fresh mint, chopped
sea salt

fills a 455 g/ 1 lb jar

Heat a non-stick frying pan/skillet over medium heat. Add the olive oil and bread, along with the garlic. Fry the bread on both sides until deeply golden. Remove the bread with a fish slice/slotted turner, sprinkle with salt and leave to drain on kitchen paper/paper towel. Discard the fried garlic from the pan (it was only in there to flavour the oil) and add the hazelnuts, rosemary and chilli. Fry until the hazelnuts have turned golden, then remove from the heat.

Roughly chop the fried bread and add to the hazelnuts, along with the orange zest and chopped mint. Stir well and season with sea salt to taste.

Pear, ginger & walnut chutney

I like a bit of crunch in my chutneys; it somehow makes them even better with cheese. Try this with a good Camembert or Vacherin.

1.2 kg/2⅔ lbs. pears, peeled, cored and quartered
300 g/11 oz. Bramley apples, peeled, cored and quartered
300 g/11 oz. onions, chopped
250 g/9 oz. fresh ginger, peeled and chopped
250 g/1⅔ cups raisins
1 teaspoon black peppercorns
2 cinnamon sticks
2 cloves
200 g/1 cup caster/granulated sugar
250 g/1¼ cups soft brown sugar
350 ml/1½ cups cider vinegar
200 g/2 cups walnuts
olive oil, for toasting

jars with airtight lids, sterillized

makes around 12 jars

Put all the ingredients except the walnuts in a large pan and bring to the boil. Simmer for 1½ hours, stirring every now and again.

In the meantime, toast the walnuts in a hot pan with a dash of olive oil until they are nicely browned all over.

Once the chutney has finished cooking, add the walnuts, pour into sterilized jars (see page 155) and store for 1–2 weeks.

Apple & cranberry chutney

Chutneys are real one-pot wonders. The most strenuous part is the sterilization (see page 155). They are very easy to experiment with, requiring only four core ingredient types: a fruit or vegetable base, sugar, vinegar and spices. The rest is free to interpretation and imagination!

This chutney works perfectly with cheese or pâté. Perfect for adding life to a sandwich, too.

1.5 kg/3⅓ lbs. Bramley apples, peeled and roughly chopped
450 g/1 lb. red onions, chopped
50 g/2 oz. fresh ginger, peeled and grated
1 teaspoon black peppercorns
1 cinnamon stick
4 cloves
250 ml/1 cup white wine vinegar
500 g/2 cups caster/superfine sugar
500 g/5½ cups cranberries, fresh or frozen

jars with airtight lids, sterillized

makes around 12 jars

OK, brace yourself. This one's quite challenging.

Put everything in a pan and bring to the boil. Reduce the heat and simmer for 1½ hours, stirring regularly.

Remove the cinnamon stick and cloves. Pour into sterilized jars (see page 155) and store in a cool, dark place for 1–2 weeks.

Raw parsnip salad with curry dressing

The poor parsnip has being playing second fiddle to the carrot for far too long. It's time to redress the balance. Slice it finely, avoiding the wooden core, and it can hold its own in any salad.

1 white onion, thinly sliced
150 ml/⅔ cup vegetable oil, plus extra for frying
1½ tablespoons curry powder
1 egg yolk
1 tablespoon mango chutney
1 teaspoon Dijon mustard
1 teaspoon white wine vinegar
freshly squeezed juice of ½ lemon
a small bunch of fresh coriander/cilantro, finely chopped
2 tablespoons warm water
4 parsnips, peeled
30 g/¼ cup cashew nuts
20 g/2 tablespoons raisins
1 sprig fresh mint, chopped
sea salt and freshly ground black pepper

a food processor

serves 4–6

Make the dressing. Fry the onion with a little vegetable oil in a frying pan/skillet until it begins to caramelize. Add the curry powder and cook for a further 2 minutes. Remove and allow to cool a little.

Put the onions in the bowl of a food processor. Add a little extra oil to the pan, scrape up the curry powder residue and add to the onions. Add the egg yolk, mango chutney, Dijon mustard and white wine vinegar. Blend to a paste. While blending, add the vegetable oil in a slow, steady stream so it emulsifies to a thick mixture. Add the lemon juice, coriander/cilantro and warm water to loosen. If it's too thick, add a little more water. Season to taste.

Using a vegetable peeler, peel the parsnips into ribbons. Discard the wooden core. Mix the parsnips with the cashews and raisins and dress liberally. Scatter with some fresh coriander/cilantro and mint leaves, and serve.

Red cabbage, beetroot, feta & apricot salad

This is a vibrant, colourful salad that marries the sweetness of ripe apricots with the saltiness of feta.

4 raw beetroot/beets, peeled
1 small red cabbage
3 spring onions/scallions
150 g/5 oz. fresh apricots, sliced
a small bunch of fresh flat leaf parsley, roughly chopped
olive oil, for dressing
150 g/5 oz. feta cheese
sea salt and freshly ground black pepper

a food processor with slicing and grating attachments

serves 6–8

Grate the beetroot/beets in the food processor using the medium grating attachment, then slice the red cabbage and spring onions using the thin slicing attachment.

Mix the all the ingredients except the feta. Season gently (remembering that feta is quite salty) and crumble the feta on top.

Tomato & basil sauce

Having a good stash of this in your freezer is a culinary game-changer. Whenever a recipe calls for canned tomatoes, substitute them with this: the difference is nothing short of miraculous. Every good Italian restaurant I know uses this sauce as the base for most of their menu. It will stain all your Tupperware a gruesome shade of golden red, but it's a small price to pay. By itself, this is one of the best pasta sauces around and makes a good tomato soup, too. In short, if there's one thing you take from this book, make it this.

150 ml/⅔ cup olive oil
10 garlic cloves, sliced
1 fresh red chilli, sliced
8 x 400-g/14-oz. cans good-quality tomatoes, chopped or whole (don't stint, it makes all the difference)
1 large bunch fresh basil, chopped
1 tablespoon salt

a hand-held electric blender

makes 800 ml/ 28 fl oz

Put the olive oil, garlic and chilli in a heavy-based pan over medium heat. Once the garlic has just got the first hint of colour, add the tomatoes, basil (stalks and all) and salt. Bring to the boil, then reduce the heat to the lowest simmer possible.

Cook for 3–4 hours, stirring frequently, until the sauce has thickened. Blitz with a hand-held blender to make a smooth sauce. Add more salt if necessary – it should be generously seasoned. Leave to cool, then store in the fridge overnight so that the flavours mature. Pour into containers and freeze for later use.

teatime

The concept of teatime is quintessentially British. It conjures up historic images of *grand dames* holding dainty china cups and tut-tutting at Churchill's billowing waistline. In reality – or at least at Megan's – teatime seems to involve a preponderance of soya lattes and good-looking media types discussing brand strategy.

What has remained, however, is the sense of indulgence that teatime foods have. Let's be honest, we don't really need to eat cake to bridge the gap between lunch and dinner – but when we do, damn, it's good!

There are a lot of great cookbooks around these days with 'healthy' cake and cookie recipes, but I'm afraid this isn't one of them. As far as I'm concerned, teatime is about lip-smacking indulgence and sugar rushes. It's about satisfying that sweet tooth that we all like to pretend we lost years ago, but which seems to reappear miraculously whenever we see the thick goo of a freshly baked brownie.

I've made a point throughout the book of insisting that you shouldn't feel too constrained by the recipes, you should experiment, mix and match. While the same is true of cakes and pastries, you can't stray too far when it comes to the cooking method – eggs need to be baked at a certain temperature to avoid scrambling them in the mix, the ratio of flour needs to be respected or you'll end up with a disgustingly sweet loaf of bread rather than a bouncy Victoria Sponge…

That said, you can (and must!) go all Willy Wonka on the toppings. In my mind, cakes shouldn't only be elegant and appetizing, they should also be fun, so make sure you have a good supply of your favourite sweets to sprinkle on top!

This is one of the very few cakes around that is genuinely dairy free. Of course, that goes out the window when you slather it with cream cheese icing like we do at Megan's, but it's still a bonus now that lactose intolerance is on the rise.

Carrot & walnut cake

180 g/1½ cups plain/ all-purpose flour
2 teaspoons baking powder
1 teaspoon bicarbonate of soda/baking soda
150 g/¾ cup caster/ superfine sugar
3 eggs
110 ml/scant ½ cup vegetable oil
2 teaspoons ground cinnamon
240 g/9 oz. carrots, grated
80 g/⅔ cup chopped walnuts
½ teaspoon lemon juice

For the icing/frosting
175 g/6 oz. cream cheese
2 tablespoons icing/ confectioners' sugar

a 20-cm/8-inch springform cake pan, greased and lined with baking parchment
a hand-held electric whisk (optional)

serves 8–10

Preheat the oven to 180°C (350°F) Gas 4.

Sift the flour, baking powder and bicarbonate of soda/baking soda together. Pour the caster/superfine sugar into a deep mixing bowl and add the eggs. Beat together for a long time, until the mixture has almost doubled in volume and is an off-white colour. A hand-held electric whisk helps.

Add the oil to the mixture, followed by the sifted dry ingredients. Fold in until it is well incorporated. Add the grated carrots, walnuts and lemon juice and fold until well mixed.

Bake in the oven for 45 minutes. You can check whether it is fully cooked by inserting a skewer – if it comes out clean, it's ready.

To make the icing/frosting, just mix the cream cheese and icing/confectioners' sugar together and spread on top of the cooled cake. You can adjust it according to your desired level of sweetness; the quantities here are just a rough guideline.

Banana & chocolate cake

This is one of the restaurant's staple cakes. We've tried all sorts of variations, but as customers keep reminding us, if it ain't broke, don't fix it. Fair enough.

180 g/1½ sticks butter, softened
190 g/scant 1 cup caster/ superfine sugar
3 eggs
3 ripe bananas, mashed
1½ teaspoons bicarbonate of soda/baking soda, dissolved in 3 teaspoons hot milk
340 g/2½ cups plain/ all-purpose flour
1½ teaspoons baking powder
200 g/7 oz. dark/bittersweet or milk/semisweet chocolate, chopped, plus extra to decorate
250 ml/1 cup whipping cream

a 25-cm/10-inch springform cake pan, greased

serves 8

Preheat the oven to 180°C (350°F) Gas 4.

Put the butter and sugar in a mixing bowl and beat with a wooden spoon or electric whisk until all the sugar has been incorporated and the mixture is pale.

Add the eggs, one at a time, mixing well between each addition to make sure it's well incorporated.

Add the mashed bananas, then the dissolved soda mixture. Mix well.

Add the flour and baking powder, folding it all in with a spoon until you have a homogeneous mixture. Fold in the chocolate.

Spoon the mixture into the prepared cake pan and bake for 40 minutes, or until a skewer inserted in the middle comes out clean. Allow the cake to cool in the pan.

Just before you are ready to serve, beat the cream to soft peaks and spread over the top of the cooled cake. Decorate with grated and shaved chocolate.

Blueberry & coconut muffins

The good old muffin: one of the most ubiquitous, well-loved breakfast treats. The base recipe remains the same, regardless of flavourings. In effect, you make your muffin mix, then add whatever you want. In this recipe it's blueberries and coconut, but pretty much anything sweet goes. Raspberries, chocolate chips, banana and cinnamon… have some fun! You can even use beetroot/beet, but don't expect anyone to buy them because they won't. Trust me.

500g/4 cups plain/ all-purpose flour
2 teaspoons baking powder
200 g/1¾ sticks butter, softened
200 g/1 cup caster/ superfine sugar
2 eggs
500 ml/2 cups whole/ full-fat milk
250 g/2 cups blueberries
40 g/½ cup sweetened desiccated coconut

a 12-hole muffin pan
a piping/pastry bag (optional)

makes 12

Preheat the oven to 180°C (350°F) Gas 4.

Prepare your muffin pan by cutting 15-cm (6-inch) squares of greaseproof/parchment paper. Find a circular object that fits snugly into each hole of the pan (a fun-size soft drink can works well), and use it to push the centre of each paper square into each section so it forms a little cup.

Sift together the flour and baking powder to remove any lumps, then set aside.

Put the butter and sugar in a large mixing bowl and beat until pale and fluffy. Add the eggs one at a time while mixing, making sure the first has been totally incorporated before adding the next. Add the milk and mix well.

Fold in the flour and baking powder until you have a thick, viscous mixture, then add the flavouring ingredients, in this case the blueberries and coconut, stirring gently so you don't crush the berries into the mixture (unless you want to, of course: it's your muffin, you can do as you please). Reserve a little coconut for sprinkling on top.

Spoon the mixture into a piping/pastry bag and pipe it into each hole, filling it about halfway up (they will grow enormously in the oven), or use a spoon.

Bake for 20 minutes, then remove and sprinkle with the remaining coconut.

A BOOK OF MODERN VERSE

I've always had a soft spot for recipes with a back story. Somehow, knowing the origins of a dish gives it a sense of grandeur, as if you're consuming a little piece of history, something that existed well before you, and will last well after you're forgotten.

This is an old Portuguese recipe given to our head chef Pedro by his cousin, who got it from his grandmother. Local folklore claims it was invented by one Francisco de Mello, a Portuguese officer who was instructed to obtain some coffee beans from French Guiana so that a plantation could be started in Brazil. The Guianan Governor, however, jealously guarded his valuable crop. Unperturbed, de Mello (who was quite the dandy), seduced the Governor's wife into giving him some coffee seeds hidden in a bouquet of flowers. Whether any of this is true is neither here nor there.

Biscuit & coffee cake

500 ml/2 cups double/ heavy cream
1 x 400-g/14-oz. can condensed milk
6 gelatine leaves
3 x 200-g/7-oz. packs plain, sweet biscuits/cookies, such as Marie or Rich Tea
450 ml/1¾ cups espresso coffee
2 tablespoons dark rum

a 25-cm/10-inch springform cake pan
a food processor (optional)

serves 8–12

Whip the cream to soft peaks (it should still be just pourable), then add the condensed milk.

Soak the gelatine in a little cold water to soften it, then remove and squeeze out any excess water. Put it in the microwave for 15 seconds until it has melted, then add to the cream mixture and stir it in.

OK, now it's time to test your bricklaying skills. Spoon some of the cream mixture into the base of the pan, about 5 mm (¼ inch) deep. Mix the coffee with the rum. Take a biscuit/cookie and dip it into the coffee mixture. Don't hang around in there or it'll get soggy. Place it on the cream base. Repeat this process until the whole base is covered. Proceed with a second layer, making sure to cover the gaps between the first layer of biscuits. Gently press the biscuits down to compact them. Spoon some more cream mixture on top and repeat the process until all the cream and 2 packs of biscuits/cookies have been used up. Make sure you end with a cream layer.

Take the remaining biscuits/cookies and crush them to a powder (the easiest way is in a food processor, but if you want to go more medieval, pop them in a bag and beat the living daylights out of them). Cover the top of the cake with the crumbs and put in the fridge for 2 hours to set.

To remove it from the pan, place a thin knife in warm water, then run it round the side of the cake. Gently release the spring and sprinkle the sides with more biscuit/cookie crumbs.

Simple strawberry cheesecake

Cheesecake is one of the few desserts that seems to cross all national boundaries. From New York bankers to Tuscan olive pickers, everyone likes a good cheesecake. This recipe sets in the fridge, so it's about as foolproof as any cake can be. That said, be careful what you leave in there with it: cheesecake absorbs odours like a sponge, as demonstrated by Megan's not-so-popular onion-scented version.

300 g/11 oz. oaty biscuits/ cookies (we use Hob Nobs)
80 g/3 oz. melted butter
3 gelatine leaves
500 g/1 lb. 2 oz. cream cheese
350 g/1½ cups natural yogurt
150 g/¾ cup caster/ superfine sugar
1 vanilla pod/bean
200 g/7 oz. strawberry jam
fresh strawberries, halved, to decorate

a 25-cm/10-inch springform cake pan
a food processor (optional)

serves 8–10

Preheat the oven to 180°C (350°F) Gas 4.

Start by making the base. Crush the biscuits to a rough powder, by hand or with a food processor. Add the melted butter, stir well and line the base of the pan with the mixture, pressing it down to compact it. Bake for 10 minutes, then remove and allow to cool.

Put the gelatine leaves in cold water to soak for 10 minutes, then remove and squeeze out any excess water. Put the now-floppy gelatine leaves in the microwave on high heat for 10 seconds to melt them.

Put the cream cheese, yogurt and caster/superfine sugar in a large mixing bowl. Halve the vanilla bean lengthwise, scrape out the seeds and add to the mixture. Discard the rest of the vanilla pod/bean. Stir well, add the liquid gelatine and stir again until it is all incorporated. Spoon the mixture onto the biscuit/cookie base, making sure it is level, and refrigerate for 30 minutes.

Arrange the halved strawberries on top, then spoon on the strawberry jam, or do it the other way round if you prefer. Return it to the fridge and leave for a hour or so.

To remove from the pan, run a sharp knife around the outside of the cake, where it meets the pan. Gently release the spring and lift out.

This is a great cookie that keeps relatively well, thanks to the honey. It also doubles up as a dessert when crumbled over vanilla ice cream with a little extra honey poured on top.

Honey & oat Anzac cookies

250 g/2 sticks plus 1 tablespoon butter, softened
35 g/2 tablespoons maple syrup
270 g/1⅓ cups demerara/turbinado sugar
350 g/2¾ cups plain/all-purpose flour
200 g/2⅔ cups desiccated coconut
230 g/scant 2½ cups oats

a large baking sheet, lined with baking parchment

makes about 15

Preheat the oven to 175°C (350°F) Gas 4.

In a large mixing bowl, mix together the butter, maple syrup and sugar. Beat for 5 minutes, until light and fluffy.

Add the flour, coconut and oats. Fold in until everything is well combined.

Use your hand to shape it into balls, approximately 70 g (3 oz.) each. Place the balls evenly on the baking sheet and push them down with your fingers until they have a flat top but are still quite thick. Make sure you leave plenty of space between them, as they will triple or quadruple in size as they cook.

Bake for 10–12 minutes, or until golden brown. Remove from the oven and allow to cool before handling.

White chocolate & pistachio cookies

Shelled pistachios are offensively expensive so you want to make the most out of them. This recipe lets their colour and flavour shine through but please make sure you use a pack of freshly opened pistachios, they have a tendency to get soft and spongy surprisingly quickly. Of course any number of other nuts will work well here. My personal favourites are macadamia and hazelnuts. I advise avoiding cashew or pine nuts, but each to their own...

350 g/2¾ cups plain/ all-purpose flour
1 teaspoon baking powder
250 g/2 sticks plus 1 tablespoon butter, softened
400 g/2 cups light brown sugar
2 eggs
a pinch of sea salt
300 g/11 oz. white chocolate chunks
80 g/¾ cup shelled pistachio nuts, roughly chopped

a stand mixer (optional)

makes 30–40

Preheat the oven to 180°C (350°F) Gas 4.

Sift the flour and baking powder together and set aside.

In a stand mixer or large mixing bowl, beat the butter with the sugar until light and fluffy. While still beating slowly, add the first egg. Once incorporated, add the second. Add the flour, baking powder and pinch of salt. Continue mixing until smooth.

You've now got your basic cookie dough, to which you could add various flavourings. You can play around at this stage to make whatever kind of cookie you like. In this case, add the white chocolate chunks and pistachios, then mix until they are evenly distributed throughout. If you don't like white chocolate, go for dark. As long as the ingredients you choose aren't too wet or mushy, you'll be fine.

Chill the mixture in the fridge for 20 minutes – this makes it easier to shape the dough without it melting and oozing through your fingers. Shape the mixture into rough balls about 40 g (1¾ oz.) each and place on a non-stick baking sheet, leaving plenty of space between the balls so that they have space to expand.

Bake for 10–15 minutes (10 for gooey, 15 for crunchy), then leave to cool on the baking sheet.

The dough freezes very well, so don't feel obliged to cook the whole batch at once.

Beta's peach, coconut & vanilla cake

I'm in awe of pastry chefs. You can play around with savoury recipes, adding a pinch of spice here, a dash of soy there, but pity the fool who tries to play God with a cake. Get the balance wrong, even a little, and you end up with something that even the bin turns its nose up at.

Some people (not me) truly have a gift with sweets, and we're very lucky to have one of them in our kitchen. Beta can bring a cake into being almost by sheer force of will. It's eerie how she can just open the pantry and create something majestic without even realizing she's doing anything special. This is one of her latest and most popular inventions.

240 g/scant 2 cups plain/ all-purpose flour
2 teaspoons baking powder
4 eggs
240 g/1¼ cups caster/ superfine sugar
70 ml/5 tablespoons vegetable oil
70 ml/5 tablespoons milk
1 tablespoon vanilla extract/vanilla bean paste
300 g/1 cup diced fresh peach, plus slices or peach jam/jelly for the top
25 g/⅓ cup sweetened desiccated coconut, plus extra to decorate

a 25-cm/10-inch springform cake pan, greased

serves 8–10

Preheat the oven to 180°C (350°F) Gas 4.

Sift the flour and baking powder together and set aside.

Beat the eggs and sugar together in a large mixing bowl until light and fluffy. While still mixing, add the vegetable oil, then the milk, and finally the vanilla extract/vanilla bean paste. Add the flour and baking powder and continue mixing until well combined.

Add the diced peach and coconut and stir well to distribute the ingredients evenly. Pour the cake mixture into the prepared pan and arrange some peach slices on the top. Sprinkle on some more coconut and bake for 45 minutes, or until a skewer comes out clean.

Allow to cool in the pan. Sprinkle with some more coconut to serve.

A special sense of pride and satisfaction goes with conserves of any sort. It's not just the act of bubbling away a cauldron of stewed fruit that's rewarding, it's those peeks into the store cupboard a few weeks down the line – you know, just to check they're doing OK.

The following recipes should be viewed only as guidelines. It's nigh on impossible to make something unpleasant, provided you stick to reasonable ingredient pairings.

The one thing you must take care over is the sterilization and storage (see below). Get this wrong and your lovingly prepared creations will turn acidic and furry in no time at all.

Apple & passion fruit jam

1 kg/2¼ lbs. Bramley apples, peeled and cored
750 g/3¾ cups caster/superfine sugar
25 passion fruits, seeds and pulp only
grated zest of 1 unwaxed lemon
1 cinnamon stick

a hand-held electric blender
jars with airtight lids, sterilized

makes 10–12 225 g/8-oz jars

Cut the apples into quarters/fourths, mix with the sugar and leave them to macerate overnight in the fridge.

Put the apples and sugar in a pan and bring to the boil. Reduce the heat to a simmer and add the passion fruit pulp, lemon zest and cinnamon. Simmer for 1 hour.

Blend with a hand-held blender until smooth. Don't worry about the seeds – they're amazingly robust and won't get blended. Transfer to sterilized jars as is, or pass through a colander to remove the seeds.

Strawberry jam

1 kg/2¼ lbs. strawberries, stalks removed and halved
750 g/3¾ cups caster/superfine sugar
grated zest of 1 unwaxed lemon
1 cinnamon stick

jars with airtight lids, sterilized

makes 10–12 225 g/8-oz jars

Sterilize the jars about 1 hour before you're ready to use them, so they'll be warm when you pour in the jam. Make sure you have tight-fitting lids. Wash the lids and jars thoroughly. Boil the lids in a pan for 10 minutes, then remove and leave to cool. Preheat the oven to 150°C (300°F) Gas 2 and put the jars in, upright, for 15 minutes, then turn the oven off and leave them in there until ready to use. Funnels also need to be sterilized in the same way; if yours is heatproof you can boil it along with the lids.

To make the jam, put the strawberries in a large bowl and add the sugar. Stir, cover with clingfilm/plastic wrap and refrigerate overnight.

Pour the mixture into a pan, add the lemon zest cinnamon and bring to the boil. Reduce to a low simmer and cook for around 1 hour. Test the consistency by pouring a little onto a cold plate: if it is still too runny, cook for a further 15 minutes, then test again.

Fill the jars when the jam is still hot, but not boiling. Pour it in and seal quickly with the lid. Turn the jars upside down and leave to cool.

Index

Acknowledgements

I have so many people to thank. Here are but a few, in no particular order.

Pedro for his tireless work and breathtaking talent. Beta, Cleo, Fernando, Daniel, and the whole Megan's kitchen team for braving hell on a daily basis and still coming out smiling. Equal thanks and respect of course to Addi, Bruno and Raul, Megan's Wine Cellar keeps growing thanks to their skill and exceptional food.

A restaurant can have the best food in the world, but without good, friendly service, it's not worth a penny. Huge thanks to Luiz for being the most professional, inspirational and cheeky Manager in the world. To Gosia for being the most passionate, fun-loving and loud Manager in the world. To Marco for being the most dedicated, resourceful and charming Manager in the world. To Don for taking immeasurable pride in both his work and Megan's itself (without you our famous garden would be a desert). To all the evening team – Vanessa, Alex, Henrique and everyone else. To the day team – there are simply too many to name but a special thanks to Alessia, Katerina, Patrick, Esti, Ioannis, Karola, Giovanni, Fernando and Eleanor.

Of course, none of this would have been possible without the support of my family and friends. I really could go on forever here so I'll try and keep it brief. Thanks to my mother for introducing me to the magic of food, my father for encouraging me to follow my passion, my brother and sister for their ability to find endless spurious reasons to visit Megan's and support me. The Kaempfers, Kian, Janah and Tom for their friendship and support over these past 4 years at Megan's and the 28 that came before. There are hundreds more who I owe thanks to – you know who you are and I'm sure you'll remind me when you notice your name's not here! I wish I could thank everybody but that would be a whole (incredibly uncommercial) book unto itself.

I did say that this was in no particular order but it's not strictly true – one stand-alone thanks goes to Amelia, whose love and support makes all life's lows lose their depth and life's highs soar that much further.